READ TO SUCCEED

Strategies for Reading Comprehension

1

INTRODUCTION

Welcome to ***READ TO SUCCEED*** *— Strategies for Reading Comprehension*. This book is the first of two volumes in a series designed for learners looking to improve their reading comprehension skills. The ability to read English quickly and effectively is crucial for scoring well on important exams such as the GEPT, TOEIC, and TOEFL. It is also an increasingly valuable skill to have on the job. This book gives learners a chance to develop skills while taking pleasure in reading at the same time.

READ TO SUCCEED *— Strategies for Reading Comprehension* will introduce you to a variety of topics. Each unit includes a main passage and a related one for those who want to make an extra effort to elevate their reading comprehension.

Each unit of ***READ TO SUCCEED*** *— Strategies for Reading Comprehension* has clearly stated objectives about which reading and vocabulary skills English learners are intended to develop. We will help students learn to grasp the main point of a passage by skimming and scanning. We will also assist students in developing their ability to draw conclusions and make inferences, to compare and contrast, and to understand the purpose for which a passage is written. Tricky topics such as collocations, context clues, words with different meanings, and nouns that can be used as adjectives will also be covered.

READ TO SUCCEED *— Strategies for Reading Comprehension* is separated into 12 units. We start by examining the world's most extreme Marathons. From there, we move on to look at tattoos, especially the history and the meanings of them over the years. The next few units will take you to the beautiful islands in Japan and stunning mountain ranges in Africa, the Himalayas, and Switzerland. Later on, we explore ways to save the earth and its wildlife, learn about some of the world's most well-known mysteries, and take a closer look at the effects that different foods have on our bodies and life spans.

Come along with us as we embark on a journey of reading. When it's all over, you will have greatly improved your English comprehension and vocabulary, and you'll have learned about a variety of cultures across the globe — all without ever having to step on a plane!

CONTENTS

CONTENT CHART

LEARNING OVERVIEW

	Word	Definition
1		0
2		a long race
3		less than
4		someone who plays sports
5		to go from one side to the other side
6		land where it is always hot and dry
7		a mountain
8		how hot or cold a place is

Before We Read
provides background knowledge related to the topic through short passages and various kinds of activities. Students can scan the main reading passage and prepare for the lesson.

THINK ABOUT IT
provides topic related picture and questions for students. The questions help students focus on the topic and provoke their prior knowledge about the topic.

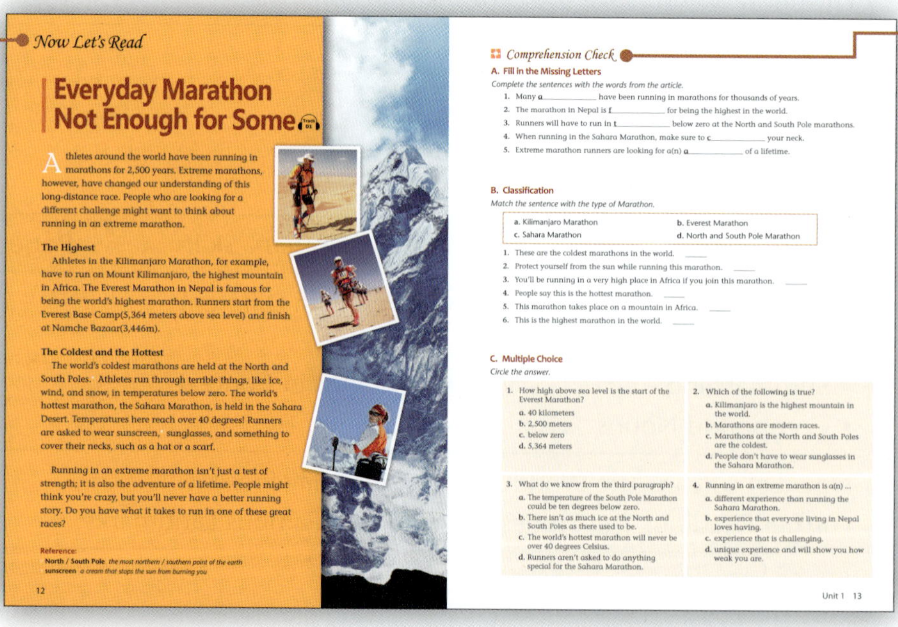

Comprehension Check
asks students about topic, main idea, and details of the main passage. Students can check their understanding about the passage through many kinds of questions like Fill in the Blanks, Classification, True or False, and Multiple Choice, etc.

Now Let's Read
presents a fascination articles to students. Students have interests on various facts like people, animals, places, things and events and enable to broaden their knowledge as well.

Vocabulary Check
confirms students' knowledge of the key words and helps students expand their vocabulary.

Reading Strategy
provides reading strategies in each unit. Students can study about Comparing and Contrasting, Drawing Conclusion, Making Inferences, and Paraphrasing, etc.

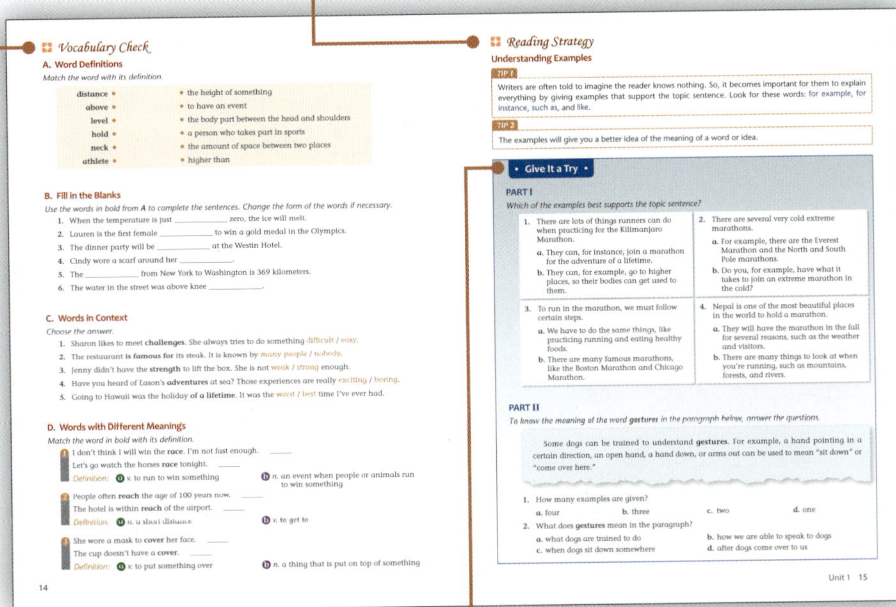

Give It a Try
provides practice about *Reading Strategy* above. Students can check their understanding about the reading strategy of the unit.

Comprehension Check
checks students' understanding about *Further Reading* through various kinds of questions.

Further Reading
presents extended reading passage connected to the main reading passage. Students can improve their reading skill through this extra passage.

UNIT 1 The World's Most Extreme Marathons

THINK ABOUT IT

Discuss with a partner.

1. What's the most difficult thing you have ever done?
2. Do you enjoy watching or running the marathon?
3. Do you know where the marathon started?
4. Have you ever met someone who has run the marathon?

Before We Read

A. Read and Answer

What do you know about these two places? Read and discuss with the class.

Mt. Everest, in the Himalayas, sits between Nepal and China.

Mount Everest stands at 8,848 meters. It is the tallest mountain in the world and it continues to grow every year! It is as tall as 23 Empire State Buildings. The **temperature** at the top can be as low as 60 degrees **below zero** Celsius.

The Sahara Desert covers much of North Africa.

The Sahara **Desert** is one of the largest deserts in the world. It is about the size of the United States. **Marathon** runner Charlie Engle was the first American **athlete** to **cross** the Sahara Desert. It took him 111 days to finish his run.

Write the words in bold above in the appropriate space. Change the form of the words if necessary.

	Word	Definition
1		0
2		a long race
3		less than
4		someone who plays sports
5		to go from one side to the other side
6		land where it is always hot and dry
7		a mountain
8		how hot or cold a place is

B. Make Predictions

Read the title, the first paragraph, and the subtitles on page 12. Answer the questions.

1. What do you think the reading is about?
   - ☐ Kilimanjaro, the highest mountain in Africa
   - ☐ how cold the North and South Poles are
   - ☐ different kinds of marathons
   - ☐ athletes running through ice

2. What does **extreme** mean in the first paragraph?
   ☐ very difficult ☐ complete ☐ boring ☐ famous

Everyday Marathon Not Enough for Some

Athletes around the world have been running in marathons for 2,500 years. Extreme marathons, however, have changed our understanding of this long-distance race. People who are looking for a different challenge might want to think about running in an extreme marathon.

The Highest

Athletes in the Kilimanjaro Marathon, for example, have to run on Mount Kilimanjaro, the highest mountain in Africa. The Everest Marathon in Nepal is famous for being the world's highest marathon. Runners start from the Everest Base Camp(5,364 meters above sea level) and finish at Namche Bazaar(3,446m).

The Coldest and the Hottest

The world's coldest marathons are held at the North and South Poles.* Athletes run through terrible things, like ice, wind, and snow, in temperatures below zero. The world's hottest marathon, the Sahara Marathon, is held in the Sahara Desert. Temperatures here reach over 40 degrees! Runners are asked to wear sunscreen,* sunglasses, and something to cover their necks, such as a hat or a scarf.

Running in an extreme marathon isn't just a test of strength; it is also the adventure of a lifetime. People might think you're crazy, but you'll never have a better running story. Do you have what it takes to run in one of these great races?

Reference:

* **North / South Pole** *the most northern / southern point of the earth*
* **sunscreen** *a cream that stops the sun from burning you*

Comprehension Check

A. Fill in the Missing Letters

Complete the sentences with the words from the article.

1. Many a____________ have been running in marathons for thousands of years.
2. The marathon in Nepal is f____________ for being the highest in the world.
3. Runners will have to run in t____________ below zero at the North and South Pole marathons.
4. When running in the Sahara Marathon, make sure to c____________ your neck.
5. Extreme marathon runners are looking for a(n) a____________ of a lifetime.

B. Classification

Match the sentence with the type of Marathon.

a. Kilimanjaro Marathon	**b.** Everest Marathon
c. Sahara Marathon	**d.** North and South Pole Marathon

1. These are the coldest marathons in the world. ______
2. Protect yourself from the sun while running this marathon. ______
3. You'll be running in a very high place in Africa if you join this marathon. ______
4. People say this is the hottest marathon. ______
5. This marathon takes place on a mountain in Africa. ______
6. This is the highest marathon in the world. ______

C. Multiple Choice

Circle the answer.

1. How high above sea level is the start of the Everest Marathon?
   - **a.** 40 kilometers
   - **b.** 2,500 meters
   - **c.** below zero
   - **d.** 5,364 meters

2. Which of the following is true?
   - **a.** Kilimanjaro is the highest mountain in the world.
   - **b.** Marathons are modern races.
   - **c.** Marathons at the North and South Poles are the coldest.
   - **d.** People don't have to wear sunglasses in the Sahara Marathon.

3. What do we know from the third paragraph?
   - **a.** The temperature of the South Pole Marathon could be ten degrees below zero.
   - **b.** There isn't as much ice at the North and South Poles as there used to be.
   - **c.** The world's hottest marathon will never be over 40 degrees Celsius.
   - **d.** Runners aren't asked to do anything special for the Sahara Marathon.

4. Running in an extreme marathon is a(n) ...
   - **a.** different experience than running the Sahara Marathon.
   - **b.** experience that everyone living in Nepal loves having.
   - **c.** experience that is challenging.
   - **d.** unique experience and will show you how weak you are.

Vocabulary Check

A. Word Definitions

Match the word with its definition.

distance •	• the height of something
above •	• to have an event
level •	• the body part between the head and shoulders
hold •	• a person who takes part in sports
neck •	• the amount of space between two places
athlete •	• higher than

B. Fill in the Blanks

*Use the words in bold from **A** to complete the sentences. Change the form of the words if necessary.*

1. When the temperature is just ____________ zero, the ice will melt.
2. Lauren is the first female ____________ to win a gold medal in the Olympics.
3. The dinner party will be ____________ at the Westin Hotel.
4. Cindy wore a scarf around her ____________.
5. The ____________ from New York to Washington is 369 kilometers.
6. The water in the street was above knee ____________.

C. Words in Context

Choose the answer.

1. Sharon likes to meet **challenges**. She always tries to do something difficult / easy.
2. The restaurant **is famous for** its steak. It is known by many people / nobody.
3. Jenny didn't have the **strength** to lift the box. She is not weak / strong enough.
4. Have you heard of Eason's **adventures** at sea? Those experiences are really exciting / boring.
5. Going to Hawaii was the holiday **of a lifetime**. It was the worst / best time I've ever had.

D. Words with Different Meanings

Match the word in bold with its definition.

1
I don't think I will win the **race**. I'm not fast enough. _____
Let's go watch the horses **race** tonight. _____
Definition: ⓐ *v.* to run to win something ⓑ *n.* an event when people or animals run to win something

2
People often **reach** the age of 100 years now. _____
The hotel is within **reach** of the airport. _____
Definition: ⓐ *n.* a short distance ⓑ *v.* to get to

3
She wore a mask to **cover** her face. _____
The cup doesn't have a **cover**. _____
Definition: ⓐ *v.* to put something over ⓑ *n.* a thing that is put on top of something

Reading Strategy

Understanding Examples

TIP 1

Writers are often told to imagine the reader knows nothing. So, it becomes important for them to explain everything by giving examples that support the topic sentence. Look for these words: for example, for instance, such as, and like.

TIP 2

The examples will give you a better idea of the meaning of a word or idea.

• Give It a Try •

PART I

Which of the examples best supports the topic sentence?

1. There are lots of things runners can do when practicing for the Kilimanjaro Marathon.
   a. They can, for instance, join a marathon for the adventure of a lifetime.
   b. They can, for example, go to higher places, so their bodies can get used to them.

2. There are several very cold extreme marathons.
   a. For example, there are the Everest Marathon and the North and South Pole marathons.
   b. Do you, for example, have what it takes to join an extreme marathon in the cold?

3. To run in the marathon, we must follow certain steps.
   a. We have to do the same things, like practicing running and eating healthy foods.
   b. There are many famous marathons, like the Boston Marathon and Chicago Marathon.

4. Nepal is one of the most beautiful places in the world to hold a marathon.
   a. They will have the marathon in the fall for several reasons, such as the weather and visitors.
   b. There are many things to look at when you're running, such as mountains, forests, and rivers.

PART II

*To know the meaning of the word **gestures** in the paragraph below, answer the questions.*

> Some dogs can be trained to understand **gestures**. For example, a hand pointing in a certain direction, an open hand, a hand down, or arms out can be used to mean "sit down" or "come over here."

1. How many examples are given?
   a. four b. three c. two d. one
2. What does **gestures** mean in the paragraph?
   a. what dogs are trained to do
   b. how we are able to speak to dogs
   c. when dogs sit down somewhere
   d. after dogs come over to us

The Marathon Through Time

Track 02

The history of the marathon goes back to 490 B.C. Back then, a young Greek soldier named Phidippides ran 42 kilometers to bring news of victory from the town of Marathon to Athens. According to* legend,* he died after delivering his message. The first marathon was held at the modern Olympic Games in 1896 in Greece to honor Phidippides. Today, the Athens Marathon is one of the most popular marathons in the world.

Photo: corono

The London Marathon has taken place each year since 1981, usually in April. Runners go along the River Thames. It is the only marathon that crosses from the eastern to western hemisphere.*

The Boston Marathon and London Marathon are also popular marathons. Too many people want to run in these marathons, so it might be hard to get into them. Don't worry though. There are lots of marathons around the world, and some are a lot of fun. The Disney Marathon, for instance, is held in January. Runners get to run through all four of the parks at Walt Disney World in Orlando, Florida. The Rock 'n' Roll Las Vegas Marathon is also a fun run. The event includes live music. It also has runners who wear Elvis Presley clothes.

Long-distance running has been popular for 2,500 years. With more and more runners doing marathons each year, this is one event that is sure to continue into the future for many more years to come.

Reference:

- * **according to** *as shown or told by something or someone*
- * **legend** *an old, well-known story*
- * **hemisphere** *one of two parts of the world*

Comprehension Check

A. Words with Different Meanings

Match the word in bold with its definition.

1. His last **name** is Blair. ______
   He had a friend **named** Morris. ______
   Definition: ⓐ *v.* to give someone a name ⓑ *n.* what someone is called

2. It is a great **honor** to meet you. ______
   Two police officers have been **honored** for their courage. ______
   Definition: ⓐ *v.* to show respect for someone ⓑ *n.* something that makes you feel proud

3. Let's go to the beach and have some **fun**. ______
   Basketball is a really **fun** sport. ______
   Definition: ⓐ *adj.* enjoyable ⓑ *n.* a very nice experience or activity

4. The band will hold a **live** concert tomorrow. ______
   He **lives** just next door to me. ______
   Definition: ⓐ *adj.* seen with your own eyes when something happens ⓑ *v.* to have your home somewhere

B. Multiple Choice

Circle the answer.

1. How long have people been enjoying long-distance running?
   a. since 1896
   b. for 2,500 years
   c. 42 years ago
   d. about 490 years ago

2. Why did Phidippides run so far?
   a. to tell people about winning something
   b. to try to get a message
   c. to tell people about losing something
   d. to become stronger

3. When did Phidippides die?
   a. before he got to the town of Marathon
   b. when he left Athens a long time ago
   c. when he was fighting as a soldier
   d. after he told people the important news

4. Which of the following is true?
   a. The Boston Marathon is very popular.
   b. The Disney Marathon is held in summer.
   c. The Las Vegas Marathon is serious.
   d. Walt Disney ran in the marathon every year.

5. Why is the marathon in Las Vegas enjoyable?
   a. The runners will play live music.
   b. The runners get to see Mickey Mouse.
   c. The runners wear costumes.
   d. The runners all go to Disney World after the marathon.

UNIT 2 Tattoos

The Guinness Book of World Records says Tom Leppard of Scotland has the most tattoos in the world. A design that looks like an animal's skin covers 99.9 percent of Leppard's body. Only the skin inside of his ears and between his toes has no tattoos.

THINK ABOUT IT

Discuss with a partner.

1. What do you think about tattoos? Do you feel they're cool?
2. Do you have a tattoo now? Have you ever had a temporary tattoo?
3. Can you think of any sports or movie stars who have unique tattoos?

Before We Read

A. Read and Answer

The 90-year-old **Atayal** woman in the picture had a **tattoo** on her face. At one time, every Atayal woman had to go through this between the ages of five and 15. Tattoos had an important **meaning**. Those without **facial** tattoos were not seen as **grown-ups**. Now, there are fewer than ten Atayal women left with facial tattoos.

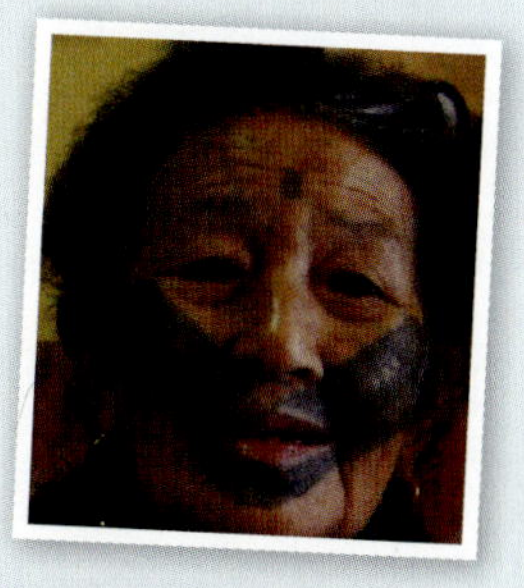

Write the words in bold above in the appropriate space. Change the form of the words if necessary.

	Word	Definition
1		an adult
2		on your face
3		one of the first groups to live in Taiwan
4		a design drawn on someone's skin in a special way
5		the idea of something

Use the words in bold above to complete the sentences. Change the form of the words if necessary.

1. Head-hunting is an old custom of the ______________ people.
2. My parents treat me like a(n) ______________. They always let me make my own decisions.
3. Lily uses ______________ cream every night for her skin.
4. I don't understand the ______________ of the painting. Could you explain it to me?
5. He had a(n) ______________ on his left arm.

B. Make Predictions

Read the title, the subtitles, and the first sentence of each paragraph on page 20. Answer the questions.

1. What do you think the reading is about?
   - ☐ what tattoos are the most popular
   - ☐ how people are tattooed
   - ☐ why people get tattoos
   - ☐ where people get ideas for tattoos

2. People have had tattoos because of all of the following BUT ...
   - ☐ they think tattoos are fashionable.
   - ☐ tattoos are a sign of importance.
   - ☐ they think tattoos are popular.
   - ☐ tattoos are important in their culture.

Now Let's Read

Body Art

Track 03

These days, tattoos are fashionable. We can see **them** on singers, movie stars, and athletes. Some tattoos are beautiful designs, just like art. Other tattoos are words that tell us something. Tattoos have been around for a long time. Over the years, people have been tattooed for many reasons.

Social Position

In the past, tattoos showed someone's position in society. In Maori culture, for example, only brave people got tattoos. During the 1800s in Europe, tattoos were popular with kings and queens. However, tattoos have also been used to mark people of a low position. Both the Greeks and Romans tattooed slaves and criminals. In Japan, tattoos were put on thieves.

Special Meanings

In many cultures, tattoos had a special meaning. Among the Atayal people in Taiwan, men were tattooed after they learned to hunt. Women got tattoos when they could make clothes. People without tattoos could not get married.

Modern Fashion

Today, people get tattoos just because they like them. Tattoos aren't very expensive, and you can get one in just a few hours. But be careful — a tattoo lasts forever. What looks beautiful now might not look beautiful in 50 years.

Comprehension Check

A. Classification

Match the people with their perception of tattoos.

a. a high social position	**1.** modern people _____
b. crime	**2.** Maori people _____
c. fashion	**3.** Europeans in the 1800s _____
d. being brave	**4.** the early Greeks and Romans _____
e. becoming an adult	**5.** the Atayal people _____

B. True or False

*Check **True** or **False**.*

		True	False
1.	Tattoos aren't very fashionable anymore.	☐	☐
2.	In Maori culture, only people who were not afraid could be tattooed.	☐	☐
3.	People who broke the law in Rome and Greece were tattooed.	☐	☐
4.	Atayal women could not get a tattoo before learning how to cook.	☐	☐
5.	These days, tattoos cost a lot of money.	☐	☐

C. Multiple Choice

Circle the answer.

1. What does **them** refer to in the first paragraph?
   a. people
   b. movie stars
   c. tattoos
   d. sports

2. People in Maori culture might get a tattoo for all of the following BUT ...
   a. saving someone's life.
   b. fighting in a war.
   c. protecting their family from their enemies.
   d. being a criminal.

3. What did both the Japanese and the Greeks tattoo to?
   a. their kings and queens
   b. unmarried people
   c. bad people
   d. slaves

4. Among the Atayal people, why did men get tattoos?
   a. They could hunt animals.
   b. They could build houses.
   c. They could make clothes.
   d. They could become kings.

5. Which of the following is true?
   a. Tattoos still cost a lot of money.
   b. All married Atayal people had tattoos.
   c. Japanese kings and queens got tattooed.
   d. Nervous and scared Maoris got tattoos.

Vocabulary Check

A. Complete the Sentences

Fill in the blanks with the words in the box.

careful	beautiful	expensive	brave	special	fashionable

1. San Diego is a(n) ______________ city. The beaches are so nice.
2. It was ______________ of you to speak in front of so many people.
3. Do you have any ______________ plans for the weekend?
4. The watch is ______________. It costs $800.
5. Be ______________ — the floor is wet.
6. Jane has a lot of fashion sense. She's the most ______________ person I know.

B. Word Definitions

Match the word/phrase with its definition.

king •	• someone who steals things
movie star •	• someone who plays sports
slave •	• a man who rules a country
singer •	• someone who is owned by another person
queen •	• someone who sings
athlete •	• someone who acts in movies
thief •	• a woman who rules a country

C. Fill in the Blanks

Use the words in bold from ***B*** *to complete the sentences. Change the form of the words if necessary.*

1. Michael Phelps is one of the greatest Olympic ______________ in history.
2. Some ______________ broke into the house last night.
3. Alex dreamed of becoming a rock ______________.
4. Those ______________ tried to run away from their owner.
5. Henry VIII was the ______________ of England from 1509 until 1547.

D. Words in Context

Choose the answer.

1. This book is about **fashion**. It tells you what clothes are hateful / popular.
2. Did she give a **reason** for calling? Tell me why / when she called.
3. As a doctor, she holds a high **position** in society. Most people respect / ignore her.
4. When I see an important date on my calendar, I **mark** it. I usually just touch / circle it.
5. Terry is a **criminal**. He works in / robs the bank.
6. Tina and Ben will **get married** next week. We have to go to the wedding hall / supermarket at 3:00 on Saturday.

Reading Strategy

Comparing and Contrasting

TIP

We often compare or contrast two subjects when we write. When we compare, we show two things are the same. Contrasting is used to show two things are different.

The following words can help you to compare and contrast:

Compare (same)	both	also	too	as well
Contrast (different)	however	but	while	on the other hand

- People speak English in **both** America and Canada.
- In France, people speak French. People in Japan, **on the other hand**, speak Japanese.

• Give It a Try •

PART I

Read the passage.

Pamela and Melody decided to get tattoos last weekend. They both went to the same tattoo shop. However, Pamela decided to get a Chinese word tattooed on her back. Melody, on the other hand, got a tattoo of a butterfly on her leg. Pamela said getting a tattoo was painful. Melody thought it hurt too.

Today, a week later, they go to the shop again. While Melody is pleased with the color of her tattoo, Pamela thinks the ink in her tattoo is not dark enough. She tells Melody: "Your butterfly tattoo is so colorful! But the word on my back is not bright like yours."

"Well," Melody answers, "my tattoo cost more money than your tattoo. Your tattoo was cheap. My tattoo was not."

PART II

*Fill in the chart with the words above. Check **Compare** or **Contrast**.*

	Melody	Pamela	Compare	Contrast
Time	Last weekend		☐	☐
Price		Cheap	☐	☐
Design	Butterfly		☐	☐
Feeling	Painful		☐	☐
Where		On her back	☐	☐
Satisfaction		Doesn't like	☐	☐
Color	Bright		☐	☐

Natural Way to Decorate Your Body

Track 04

Henna tattooing is a special kind of body art. Henna tattoos are made from the leaves of the henna plant. They are popular because they are temporary and painless. They are not permanent marks. They **disappear** after a few weeks. It's easy to draw beautiful patterns on your skin, dye your hair, or stain your nails with henna.

People have used henna to dye their skin for thousands of years. Traditionally, henna has been used to decorate hands and feet. However, these days henna is used to dye any part of the skin. The henna artist uses a cone or a bottle to squeeze the henna onto the skin in a beautiful design. The longer the henna paste stays on the skin, the darker the tattoo will be.

Henna has been used as a hair dye for 6,000 years. Henna powder is mixed with lemon juice, orange juice, or vinegar. After a few hours, it is ready. People put the henna paste on their hair and leave it for several hours. When they wash the paste away, their hair is permanently dyed red.

One of the oldest uses of henna is fingernail painting. As with hair and skin, people make a paste with henna powder and lemon juice. They apply the paste to their nails at night. In the morning, they wash it off. A deep red stain remains on the nails.

The parts in green are areas where henna has been used for thousands of years.

Comprehension Check

A. Word Definitions

Match the word with its definition.

temporary •	• push something out from all directions
paste •	• lasting a short time
squeeze •	• lasting forever
permanent •	• change the color of something
apply •	• a mix of powder and liquid
dye •	• put on something

B. Complete the Chart

*Fill in the chart using the nouns to make adjectives with **–ful** or **–less**.*

Noun	Adjective	
pain		painless
hope	hopeful	
care	careful	
help		helpless
use	useful	

TIP
*The suffix **–less** means "without" while **–ful** means "full of." The suffixes are usually added to nouns to make adjectives.*

Use the words above to complete the sentences.

1. How is your leg? Is the cut ______________?
2. The information is ______________. It does not help us at all.
3. It was ______________ of him to break the glass.
4. I'm a little worried, but I'm ______________ that we can solve the problem.
5. My brother is very ______________. He often helps me with my homework.

C. Multiple Choice

Circle the answer.

1. Henna tattoos are popular because…
   a. they are permanent.
   b. they are painless.
   c. they are red.
   d. they wash off.

2. How was henna used traditionally?
   a. to dye every part of the body
   b. to drink with lemon juice
   c. to dye the hands and feet
   d. to color the cloth

3. What does **disappear** mean in the first paragraph?
   a. be made from
   b. go away
   c. look beautiful
   d. stay forever

4. What color does henna paste result in on hair?
   a. green
   b. blue
   c. black
   d. red

UNIT 3

A Good Laugh

THINK ABOUT IT

Discuss with a partner.

1. Do you like to listen to other people tell jokes?
2. What kinds of jokes do people in your country like?
3. Are jokes from your own language funny in English?
4. Do you know any funny people from other countries? Where are they from?

Before We Read

A. Say It Right

TIP *What do you call a bad joke in English? You can call it a **lame joke**.*

*Do you think the examples below are **lame jokes**? Discuss with your partner.*

What did the dog say to the tree?

Bark.

What's black white black white black white?

A panda rolling down the stairs.

Working in groups, come up with a lame joke. Score other groups' lame jokes below.

5 4 3 2 1 0

	Lame Joke	Score
Group A		
Group B		
Group C		

B. Scan

Read the article on page 28. What do the following numbers refer to?

1. 24 ☐ the number of times the doctor called the woman
   ☐ the number of hours the woman can live
2. 65 ☐ how fast cars can go
   ☐ the number of the road
3. 2 ☐ the number of jobs the dog had before
   ☐ the number of languages the dog can speak

C. Make Predictions

Guess what each joke is about with a partner.

① Bad News
doctor bad news only have 24 hours

② Signs of Confusion
police officer going so slowly sign speed

③ Can You Speak Another Language?
dog job ad boss laughed computer language

Now Let's Read

Funny English Jokes

Track 05

① Bad News

A doctor told a patient, "Ma'am, I have bad news and very bad news."

"Tell me the bad news first," said the patient.

"Well, you have 24 hours to live."

"24 hours? That's terrible! OK, what's the very bad news?"

"I've been trying to reach you since yesterday," answered the doctor.

② Signs of Confusion

A police officer stops a car full of women. "Miss," he says, "The speed limit is 65 kilometers per hour. Why were you going so slowly?"

"The signs said 30, not 65," replies the woman.

"Miss, that's not the speed limit. That's the name of the highway."

The officer then notices that the woman's friends are shaking badly. "Are they OK?" the officer asks. "They look frightened."

"Oh, they'll be fine in a minute," she replies. "We just got off Highway 192."

③ Can You Speak Another Language?

A dog saw a job ad in a window. He went into the company. The boss laughed and said, "I can't hire a dog."

The dog pointed to the ad. It said, "Anyone may apply."

"OK, type me a letter," said the boss. The dog went to a computer and typed a perfect letter.

"OK, I'll hire you if you can speak two languages."

The dog looked up at the boss and said, "Meow.*"

Reference:

* **meow** *the sound of a cat*

Comprehension Check

A. Classification

Match the sentence with the joke in the article.

1. The joke is about misunderstanding. ______
2. There's an animal in the story. ______
3. A group of women are in this joke. ______
4. The joke happens in a hospital. ______
5. It talks about speaking two languages. ______
6. Someone got some bad news. ______

B. Multiple Choice

Circle the answer.

1. What is another possible title for **Bad News**?
   a. Some Good Luck
   b. The Very Bad Doctor
   c. From Bad to Worse
   d. Different Patients

2. In **Bad News**, what information is NOT clear?
   a. they are talking on the telephone
   b. the very bad news about the patient
   c. how the patient feels about the news
   d. the type of news that the doctor has

3. In **Signs of Confusion**, how fast is the woman driving when the officer stops her?
   a. 65 kilometers per hour
   b. 30 kilometers per hour
   c. 192 kilometers per hour
   d. It doesn't say.

4. What can we say about the women in **Signs of Confusion**?
   a. They are having fun.
   b. They are very scared.
   c. They like going fast.
   d. They are pretty angry.

5. What do we know about the boss in **Can You Speak Another Language**?
   a. He likes cats more than any other animal.
   b. He can speak many different languages.
   c. He is hoping to find a dog for the job.
   d. He is looking for a new worker.

C. Complete the Passage

Fill in the blanks with the words in the box. Change the form of the words if necessary.

terrible	slowly	notice	frightened	laugh

Two hunters are in the woods. They are 1. ____________ and having a good time. Then, something 2. ____________ happens. One of the hunters starts walking very 3. ____________ and falls to the ground. The other hunter 4. ____________ that his friend can't move and that he might not be alive. He's 5. ____________ and calls for help on the phone. "My friend is dead!" he says. The man on the phone replies, "Take it easy. First, let's make sure he's dead." It is quiet, and a gunshot is heard. Then the hunter says, "OK, now what?"

— *Joke by Gurpal Gosall*

Vocabulary Check

A. Words with Different Meanings

Match the word in bold with its definition.

1
The doctor told the **patient** to get some rest. ______
The mother was very **patient** with her baby. ______
Definition: ⓐ *n.* a sick person ⓑ *adj.* calm, without becoming angry

2
The road **sign** says to turn right for Rock City. ______
Please **sign** here. ______
Definition: ⓐ *v.* to write your name ⓑ *n.* a board that tells you something

3
I **notice** that you got a haircut. ______
Did you see the **notice** about the meeting? ______
Definition: ⓐ *n.* information ⓑ *v.* to see

4
What **type** of movies do you like? ______
The secretary is **typing** a letter for her boss. ______
Definition: ⓐ *v.* to write something on a computer ⓑ *n.* a kind

B. Word Definitions

Match the word/phrase with its definition.

reach •	• to pay someone to do a job
speed limit •	• how fast cars can drive
highway •	• a business
company •	• a road where cars go fast
hire •	• to contact

C. Fill in the Blanks

Use the words in bold from **B** *to complete the sentences. Change the form of the words if necessary.*

1. The boss ______________ Jack as a cook last month.
2. Bob works for a computer ______________.
3. The ______________ on this road is 60 kilometers per hour.
4. The ______________ goes all the way to Alabama.
5. I can't ______________ him on his cell phone.

D. Words in Context

Choose the answer.

1. The food at the restaurant was **terrible**. You will / won't like it.
2. The new rule has caused a lot of **confusion**. I can't understand / can get it.
3. A: Did John **reply** to your question?
   B: No, he didn't say / find anything.
4. Don't be **frightened**. I'm not going to hurt / help you.
5. Chris will be here **in a minute**. You will see him tomorrow / soon.
6. She **applied** for a job. She really wants to get / leave it.

Reading Strategy

Drawing Conclusions and Making Inferences

TIP

Understanding information that is not given in the passage is called drawing conclusions and making inferences. To do this, use the information that is already in the article.

• Give It a Try •

PART I

Read the article again and answer the questions.

1. In **Bad News**, why was the very bad news worse than the bad news?
   - **a.** The doctor plays a joke on the patient.
   - **b.** The patient has less than 24 hours to live.
   - **c.** The patient likes to talk to the doctor.
   - **d.** The patient's telephone is broken.

2. In **Signs of Confusion**, why are the driver's friends afraid?
   - **a.** She is driving very slowly.
   - **b.** The officer stops the car.
   - **c.** She doesn't know the way.
   - **d.** She was driving very fast.

PART II

Read the passage and ask yourself, "What details are given? What do I already know? What information is not known?" Write your conclusion in the box.

Lizzie put her black nose on the glass door. The door opened, and Lizzie went inside. She shook herself to get the rain off. Then she jumped on the sofa. Mary told her to get off. Lizzie looked up at Mary with her tongue out. Her tail was moving quickly. Mary touched Lizzie's head and gave her a bone.

Details from the Reading:
Lizzie has a black nose. She shook herself to get dry. She moved her tail. She got a bone.

What I Already Know:
Dogs often have black noses. They shake themselves to get dry. They have tails. They like bones.

Conclusion:
Lizzie is probably a ______________.

Further Reading

Humor Around the World

Track 06

Laughter is a language that people all around the world can understand. However, a funny joke in one country might not be funny in another place. A British group decided to find out if people from different countries laugh at the same jokes. They made a website (www.laughlab.co.uk) and asked people to send in jokes and to judge others' jokes. Here were their findings:

People from Britain, Australia, and New Zealand like jokes that use words in a humorous way.

Person A: Where did your mother come from?

Person B: Alaska.

Person A: Don't bother, I'll ask her myself!

Americans and Canadians think stupid people are funny.

Q: How do you get an idiot* to laugh on Saturday?

A: Tell them a joke on Wednesday.

France, Denmark, and Belgium love strange things that are not real, like a talking animal.

A duck walks into a drugstore and tells the clerk, "Give me some lipstick* and put it on my bill!"

The group learned that the only country that liked all types of humor was Germany. So remember that wherever you travel, people might have a different sense of humor. It might take some time for you to understand their jokes. Then you can start laughing with them!

Understanding Jokes

- **Alaska** sounds like "I'll ask her."
- **Bill** can mean "a duck's mouth" or "a list showing how much you have to pay."

Reference:

* **idiot** *a stupid person*
* **lipstick** *something used to add color to your lips*

Comprehension Check

A. Complete the Sentences

Fill in the blanks with the words in the box. Change the form of the words if necessary.

interest	bore	cry	excite	confuse

1. I couldn't sleep all night because the ______________ baby was too noisy.
2. I love plays. Among them, I think Hamlet is the most ______________ play.
3. My sister can't do her homework because there are too many ______________ questions.
4. The movie doesn't have a surprising ending. It's so ______________.
5. The new roller coaster looks very ______________. I can't wait to ride it.

> TIP
> **Present Participles**
> *The present participle (V-ing) can be used as an adjective to describe a noun. Look at the examples below:*
> a **talking** animal a **laughing** woman a **boring** class

B. Fill in the Blanks

Complete the sentences with the words in parentheses. Change the form of the words if necessary.

1. We all like Pamela because she is so ______________ (humor).
2. On Christmas, children are full of ______________ (joy).
3. There is a lot of ______________ (danger) in riding a motorcycle.
4. When Sean jumped into the river to save the girl, it was a ______________ (courage) thing to do.

> TIP
> **Suffix: –ous**
> *The suffix **–ous** is usually added to nouns to make adjectives.*

C. Multiple Choice

Circle the answer.

1. Which of the following is true?
   a. People in every country like to laugh.
   b. People in only some countries like to laugh.
   c. Only Americans and Canadians like to laugh.
   d. We all seem to laugh at the same jokes.

2. Why does Person A say, **"Don't bother, I'll ask her myself?"**
   a. Person A is really interested in Alaska.
   b. Person A has actually never been to Alaska.
   c. Person A doesn't want to trouble Person B.
   d. Person A hasn't met Person B's mother.

3. How long does it take for stupid people to understand the joke?
   a. They understand it immediately.
   b. It takes them a few days.
   c. They understand it the same day.
   d. They never understand it.

4. What kind of joke would people living in France, Denmark, and Belgium enjoy?
   a. one about lipstick
   b. one about stupid people
   c. one about talking animals
   d. one about the word ketchup

UNIT 4

April Fools' Day

People get to be childish on April Fools' Day. Around the world, the day of jokes isn't always on April 1st. In Belgium, it's on December 28th. And Scotland has two days — April 1st and 2nd — to make people look stupid.

THINK ABOUT IT

Discuss with a partner.

1. Have you played tricks on people on April Fools' Day? Or have your friends played tricks on you?
2. Do you have any ideas for playing tricks on your friends?

Before We Read

A. You Might Want to Know ...

Word of the Day:

fool
a stupid person

Phrase of the Day:

play tricks / jokes on someone
to trick someone

Quote of the Day:

"The first of April is the day we remember what we are the other 364 days of the year."
— Mark Twain

B. Read and Answer

All about April Fools' Day

- Some people believe the custom of April Fools' Day began in France during the 16th **century**.
- April Fools' Day is a day to play **tricks** on people.
- If your friends believe something you **make up**, you say, "April Fools!"
- April Fools' Day is **celebrated** all over the world. In Poland, for example, the tradition is to get people wet by pouring water on them.

Write the words in bold above in the appropriate space. Change the form of the words if necessary.

	Word	Definition
1		to invent
2		a period of 100 years
3		a joke
4		to enjoy a special day

Use the words in bold above to complete the sentences. Change the form of the words if necessary.

1. Today is your birthday. Let's go out and ______________.
2. Sam is naughty and likes to play ______________ on his friends.
3. That's not true! You're just ______________ the story.
4. Basketball was invented over a ______________ ago.

C. Scan

Read the second paragraph on page 36. Answer the questions.

1. When did people celebrate the New Year in 16th century France?
2. Who made January 1st, the beginning of the New Year?
3. Why didn't all the people follow the change?

Don't Be Fooled!

If you like to play tricks on people, April Fools' Day is for you. On this day, you might tell your friends that classes have been canceled. You could also put a plastic insect in someone's drink. One famous trick was the spaghetti tree story. On the first of April 1957, a British TV program made up a story about spaghetti trees. After that, hundreds of people believed that spaghetti grew on trees.

It is thought that April Fools' Day began in France. Five centuries ago, the first day of the New Year was on April 1st. Then, in the late 1500s, Pope Gregory XIII moved New Year's Day to January 1st. However, word traveled slowly in those days, so many people didn't know about the change. Some people knew and didn't care. **They** still celebrated the New Year on April 1st.

These people were called "April fools," and other people played tricks on them to make them look silly. They sent these "fools" out to look for things that weren't there, or tried to make them believe something that wasn't true. Finally, April Fools' Day became popular all over Europe. Today, it's still a day for tricks and fun almost everywhere in the world.

Comprehension Check

A. True or False

*Check **True** or **False**.*

	True	False
1. April Fools' Day is for people who like to play tricks on other people.	☐	☐
2. On April Fools' Day 1957, a British TV program reported that spaghetti grew on trees.	☐	☐
3. Today, the first day of the New Year is on April 1st officially.	☐	☐
4. Five centuries ago, word traveled quickly.	☐	☐
5. People in many countries celebrate April Fools' Day.	☐	☐

B. Short Answers

Write the answer.

1. Q: What are some tricks we can play on people?
   A: ____________________

2. Q: What did a British TV program make a fake story about?
   A: ____________________

3. Q: Where did April Fools' Day begin?
   A: ____________________

4. Q: When was the New Year's Day changed to January 1st?
   A: ____________________

5. Q: What did people call those who kept celebrating the New Year's Day on April 1st?
   A: ____________________

C. Multiple Choice

Circle the answer.

1. What is the reading mainly about?
   a. not being fooled on April Fools' Day
   b. someone who celebrates New Year's Day
   c. the development of April Fools' Day
   d. playing a good April Fools' trick

2. Which trick is NOT described in the passage?
   a. putting something in a drink
   b. playing a trick on Pope Gregory XIII
   c. giving false information about classes
   d. making up a very crazy story

3. Why didn't everyone know that New Year's Day had been changed?
   a. It used to be hard to get information.
   b. The Pope kept the change a secret.
   c. They came from the same town in France.
   d. The people were too silly to understand.

4. What does **they** refer to in the second paragraph?
   a. people who didn't know about the change
   b. people who knew about the change
   c. people who worked for the Pope
   d. people who were born on April 1st

Vocabulary Check

A. Complete the Sentences

Fill in the blanks with the words in the box. Change the form of the words if necessary.

trick	care	drink

1. The students were playing ______________ on their teacher.
   Bill is too smart to be ______________.
2. The store sells different kinds of soft ______________.
   Could I get you something to ______________?
3. My neighbor takes ______________ of my dog while I'm away.
   Bob ______________ what other people think of him all the time.

B. Word Group

Circle the word that is not like the others.

1. bag, hamburger, **spaghetti**, pizza
2. **silly**, stupid, foolish, smart
3. soil, bug, **insect**, worm
4. wooden, **plastic**, cotton, meat

C. Fill in the Blanks

*Use the words in bold from **B** to complete the sentences. Change the form of the words if necessary.*

1. I put the fruit in the ______________ bag.
2. Some people raise ______________ as their pets.
3. That was ______________ of me. I put this shoe on the wrong foot.
4. I love all kinds of noodles, especially ______________.

D. Meanings in Context

Choose the meaning of the sentence.

a. The floor was all wet.
b. It was very crowded.
c. We don't have to go to school.
d. Wait for me a little while.
e. Many people watch the show every week.
f. Everyone knows he is getting married.

1. Classes are **canceled** tomorrow. ______
2. *The Voice* is a popular TV **program**. ______
3. I'm **almost** done with my report. ______
4. **Hundreds of** people went to the party. ______
5. News **travels** fast. ______
6. There was water **everywhere**. ______

Reading Strategy

Understanding the Topic, Main Idea, and Topic Sentence

TIP

The topic is the subject of a paragraph. We can express the topic in either a word or a phrase. The first sentence of the paragraph usually introduces the main idea. It is called the topic sentence.

- April Fools' Day is celebrated in many ways. Americans play small jokes on both their friends and people they don't know. They might put salt in their friends' tea. Portuguese people throw flour at their friends. In France, kids fool their classmates by taping paper fish to their backs.
  - **Topic:** April Fools' Day
  - **Main Idea:** Different April Fools' Day celebrations
  - **Topic Sentence:** April Fools' Day is celebrated in many ways.

• Give It a Try •

PART I

Read the passage and answer the questions.

In the next ten years, most of us will have robots for servants. They will look and act just like real people. We'll even be able to talk to these machines. Interestingly, the robots of tomorrow will learn how to serve people from experience. They won't get tired. They won't fight with us. They won't even ask for more money. Their only goal will be to make our lives more comfortable.

1. The topic of the passage is ______________.
2. Choose the topic sentence of the passage.
   - **a.** In the next ten years, most of us will have robots for servants.
   - **b.** We'll even be able to talk to these machines.
   - **c.** Interestingly, the robots of tomorrow will learn how to serve people from experience.
   - **d.** They won't fight with us.

PART II

Read the passage and answer the questions.

In his free time, Jorge enjoys playing all kinds of games. His favorite game is chess. Jorge loves how chess makes him think. Jorge also likes to play Monopoly. He thinks the game is a lot of fun because it needs both luck and skill. If he's alone, Jorge usually plays video games. He is interested in almost every kind of video game. He just doesn't like violent games.

1. The topic of the passage is ______________.
2. Choose the main idea of the passage.
   - **a.** Jorge dislikes violence.
   - **b.** Jorge likes to think.
   - **c.** Jorge enjoys Monopoly.
   - **d.** Jorge enjoys playing games.

Further Reading

Believe It or Not

Smell-o-Vision

In 1965, the BBC reported the invention of "smell-o-vision." Smell-o-vision allowed audiences to smell odors from TV programs. They showed this new invention by cutting onions and making coffee on TV. Many viewers later said that they had smelled these odors in their homes.

The Left-Handed Whopper

In 1998, Burger King ran an advertisement of a "left-handed Whopper." The Whopper was a special hamburger designed for left-handed people. Thousands of people went to the restaurant and said they wanted to buy the new Whopper.

Cook From Your Car

An advertisement by BMW in 2004 said their SHEF Technology allowed drivers to cook dinners from their cars while driving home. All dials for the home oven were built into the car. BMW even offered chicken recipes for drivers.

Plan Your Mars Vacation

In 2009, the travel website Expedia offered flights to Mars at a price of only $99. It claimed you could save over $3,000,000,000,000 on a trip to Mars.

Comprehension Check

A. Word Definitions

Match the word with its definition.

odor •	• new machines or ways of doing things
left-handed •	• to say that something is true
technology •	• a way to cook food
recipe •	• a smell
claim •	• using the left hand rather than the right hand for activities

B. Group Work

Discuss the following questions with your partner and share the answers with the class.

1. Q: What kinds of food have a strong **odor**?
   A: ____________________

2. Q: How many famous **left-handed** people can you name?
   A: ____________________

3. Q: What are five forms of **technology** you use regularly?
   A: ____________________

C. Multiple Choice

Circle the answer.

1. Which of the following is true?
   a. Viewers could smell the onions and coffee.
   b. Viewers thought they could smell the onions and coffee.
   c. Viewers could not actually see the onions and coffee.
   d. Viewers didn't think they could smell the onions and coffee.

2. Why did thousands of people go to Burger King?
   a. to try out the new menu
   b. to get a cheaper Whopper
   c. to see the funny advertisement
   d. to meet left-handed people

3. BMW offered all of the following BUT ...
   a. a way to cook a chicken dish.
   b. dials for home ovens in the cars.
   c. a way for drivers to turn on their home ovens.
   d. special prices on some of their chicken dishes.

4. What is another appropriate title for the reading?
   a. BMW Fools People Again
   b. Trips to Mars in the Future
   c. Famous April Fools' Jokes
   d. April Fools' Day in Different Countries

UNIT 5 Food for Thought

When people think of Chinese food, they think of it. The person who invented it probably got the idea from the Chinese tradition of putting messages in cakes. It is found in Chinese restaurants in North America. Can you guess what it is?

THINK ABOUT IT

Discuss with a partner.

1. Name some different desserts that you like.
2. Do you believe what the fortune inside the cookie says?
3. What kind of fortune would you like to receive?

Before We Read

A. Read and Answer

People like these sweet and **crunchy** snacks. It's **fun** to break open the cookies because there are **fortunes** in them. The piece of paper gives people **advice** or says something funny. The **lucky** numbers inside might help you to win the **lottery**.

Write the words in bold above in the appropriate space. Change the form of the words if necessary.

	Word	Definition
1		a suggestion
2		making a noise when you bite it
3		enjoyable
4		what happens to a person: good or bad luck
5		having good luck
6		a game for making money

Use the words in bold above to complete the sentences. Change the form of the words if necessary.

1. Skiing is a ______________ sport.
2. I like really ______________ cereal, so I don't put milk on it.
3. I never buy ______________ tickets. I don't believe in luck.
4. My father sometimes gives me ______________ on matters.
5. The woman at the night market told me my ______________ with cards.
6. We are ______________ to have our own house.

B. Match

Look at these fortune cookie sayings. Match the sentence parts.

The time is right •	• with a single step.
You will be invited to •	• believing.
A journey of a thousand miles begins •	• an exciting event.
Seeing is •	• to make new friends.
Before you receive, •	• the lucky and the brave.
A good beginning is •	• you must give.
Love is for •	• half the task.

A Lucky Dessert

It looks like a dumpling, but you eat **it** after your meal. It's sweet and crunchy and has a little piece of paper inside. What is it? It's a fortune cookie.

Most people think eating fortune cookies is a Chinese custom. After all, these little snacks are served in Chinese restaurants. Fortune cookies were actually invented in America. Who invented them is still a mystery. Chinese immigrants in California began making them in the early 20th century. Everyone liked these fun, sweet snacks **they** made, and the idea quickly caught on.

Now fortune cookies are popular in Chinese restaurants all across America. People can hardly wait to open them and read their fortunes. Some fortunes are funny, like "You love fortune cookies." **Others** may include advice, wise sayings, or even lucky numbers.

A few fortune cookies are very lucky. In 2005, 110 people bought lottery tickets with the same five numbers — 22, 28, 32, 33, and 39 — and won 19 million dollars! How did **they** choose these lucky numbers? From fortunes inside fortune cookies.

Over three billion fortune cookies are produced each year. Maybe the next time you eat **one**, it will be your lucky day.

Comprehension Check

A. Main Idea

Write the number of the paragraph to match each topic.

1. Actually fortune cookies were not invented in China. ______
2. Some fortune cookies are very lucky. ______
3. People like to read various messages in fortune cookies. ______

B. Reference Word

Choose what the word in bold refers to.

1. **it** (Paragraph 1)	**a.** a dumpling	**b.** a piece of paper	**c.** a fortune cookie
2. **they** (Paragraph 2)	**a.** snacks	**b.** Chinese immigrants	**c.** inventions
3. **others** (Paragraph 3)	**a.** fortunes	**b.** fortune cookies	**c.** restaurants
4. **they** (Paragraph 4)	**a.** lottery winners	**b.** lottery tickets	**c.** numbers
5. **one** (Paragraph 5)	**a.** a day	**b.** each year	**c.** a cookie

C. Summary

Choose the answer.

Fortune cookies are eaten all **1.** ____________ America. Many people think fortune cookies are a **2.** ____________ from China because they're **3.** ____________ in Chinese restaurants. But fortune cookies were actually invented in America. Chinese immigrants started making them over 100 years ago. Everyone liked these sweet snacks, and the idea started to **4.** ____________.

1. **a.** without	**b.** for	**c.** toward	**d.** across
2. **a.** law	**b.** secret	**c.** custom	**d.** rule
3. **a.** served	**b.** sent	**c.** taken	**d.** rested
4. **a.** catching on	**b.** catch on	**c.** catches on	**d.** caught on

D. Multiple Choice

Circle the answer.

1. Where are fortune cookies popular?
   a. all over America
   b. just in California
   c. in China
   d. at lottery ticket shops

2. Fortunes are all of the following BUT ...
   a. funny.
   b. smart.
   c. lucky.
   d. sad.

3. What did the lucky people win in 2005?
   a. They won some fortune cookies.
   b. They won some more tickets.
   c. They won an amount of money.
   d. They won a new restaurant.

4. Who invented fortune cookies?
   a. immigrants from China
   b. nobody knows
   c. lottery ticket sellers
   d. an American restaurant owner

Vocabulary Check

A. Complete the Chart

Fill in the chart using the base form of the verbs.

Base Form	choose	win	catch	eat	buy
Past Tense					
Past Participle					

Complete the sentences with the words above.

1. They ______________ Ben to be the class leader.
2. I am glad that you ______________ the game.
3. She has ______________ a bad cold.
4. I ______________ dumplings for lunch today.
5. I ______________ those pants on sale last week.

B. Word Definitions

Match the word with its definition.

sweet •	• a tradition
custom •	• to provide food or drink
serve •	• to design or think of something new
invent •	• having sugar
produce •	• to make

C. Fill in the Blanks

*Use the words in bold from **B** to complete the sentences. Change the form of the words if necessary.*

1. The ______________ of Christmas cards probably started in Britain in 1840.
2. The airplane was ______________ by the Wright brothers.
3. Breakfast is ______________ until 10:30.
4. You put in too much sugar. This tea is very ______________.
5. The factory ______________ 2,000 cars a day.

D. Words in Context

Choose the answer.

1. He has houses **all across** the country. You can find one in main / every state.
2. I **can hardly wait to** try the new restaurant. It must be good / bad.
3. A lot of Asian **immigrants** came to / from America during the last two centuries.
4. This new fashion is **catching on**. Everyone loves / hates it.
5. His death is still a **mystery**. Everyone / No one knows what happened.

Reading Strategy

Paraphrasing

TIP

Paraphrasing is when you use another writer's ideas. Remember you must write in your own words. Don't forget to include the main idea.

• Give It a Try •

PART I

Go back to the article. Which of the following passages best retells the ideas of the second paragraph?

a Fortune cookies look like dumplings, but they are sweet and crunchy. They also have a small piece of paper inside and are served as dessert. This means that they are eaten after a meal. Fortune cookies are very popular in Chinese restaurants across America.

b Many people think that fortune cookies come from China because they are served in Chinese restaurants. Fortune cookies were invented in America. Americans liked them, so they became popular in the United States. Americans have been eating them for over 100 years.

PART II

Paraphrase the passage below.

My Own Cookie makes special fortune cookies. Each cookie is fresh and delicious. Fortune cookies are usually sweet, but our fortune cookies are not. Therefore, they won't make you fat. We have great fortune cookies for birthdays, weddings, and even holidays. On Valentine's Day, we make red fortune cookies that look like hearts. What kind of fortune cookie are you looking for? Maybe we can help you. Give us a call or check our website: www.myowncookie.com.

Inventing Foods by Accident

Track 10

Sandwiches

The sandwich is named after the Fourth Earl* of Sandwich. As the story goes, the earl was too busy playing cards to stop for dinner. So, he ordered beef between two slices of bread. This way, he could continue. Later, the sandwich became popular. Luckily, we have more choices than just beef and bread.

Potato Chips

Potato chips were created in 1853 at a New York hotel. A customer complained that the fried potatoes were thick. So, the cook decided to teach the customer a lesson. He cut the potatoes so thin that they couldn't be eaten with a fork. The guest loved them. Soon, the chips were added to the hotel's menu and the rest is history.

Ice Cream Cones

Ernest Hamwi was selling waffles* at the World's Fair in 1904. When the ice cream seller next to him ran out of paper cups, Hamwi used a waffle to make a cone. Several years earlier, Italo Marchiony pushed an ice cream cart on wall street. Customers often broke his glass cups, so he invented an edible waffle cone to hold his ice cream. Hamwi's ice cream cones and Marchioni's cones looked different, so many people say they both invented the ice cream cone separately.

Donuts

People say a sailor named Hanson Gregory invented the donut. One day, Gregory's mother made a kind of oily cake for him to take on a ship. One story goes that Gregory needed both hands to control the ship in a storm, so he put the donut on the wheel. When he took it off, it had a hole. Gregory said it tasted better like that. Today, every donut has a hole.

Reference:

* **earl** *a man with a high social position*
* **waffle** *a kind of cake people eat for breakfast*

Comprehension Check

A. Match

Match the cause and effect.

Effect

a. So he used a waffle to make a cone.
b. So he ordered beef between two slices of bread.
c. So he put the donut on the wheel.
d. So the cook cut the potatoes very thin.

Cause

1. The Fourth Earl of Sandwich was busy playing cards. ______
2. A customer complained that the fried potatoes were thick. ______
3. An ice cream seller ran out of paper cups. ______
4. A sailor needed both hands to control the ship in a storm. ______

B. Measure Words

Write the measure word in the blank. Some blanks have more than one answer.

scoop	cup	piece	slice	glass

1.

a __________ of cheese

2.

a __________ of ice cream

3.

a __________ of milk

4.

a __________ of bread

5.

a __________ of coffee

6.

a __________ of cake

C. Multiple Choice

Circle the answer.

1. All of these foods were created ...
a. secretly.
b. by chance.
c. over many years.
d. in New York.

2. Why did the cook cut the potatoes so thin?
a. He was unhappy with the customer.
b. He wanted to make the customer happy.
c. He knew the customer had a fork.
d. He didn't understand the customer.

3. Ernest Hamwi used a waffle to make a cone because ...
a. somebody ran away with the paper cups.
b. he saw Italo Marchiony use paper cups.
c. the ice cream seller didn't have any paper cups.
d. they were popular at the World's Fair.

4. Where was Hanson Gregory when he invented the donut?
a. in his mother's home
b. at a cake shop
c. in a car
d. on the ocean

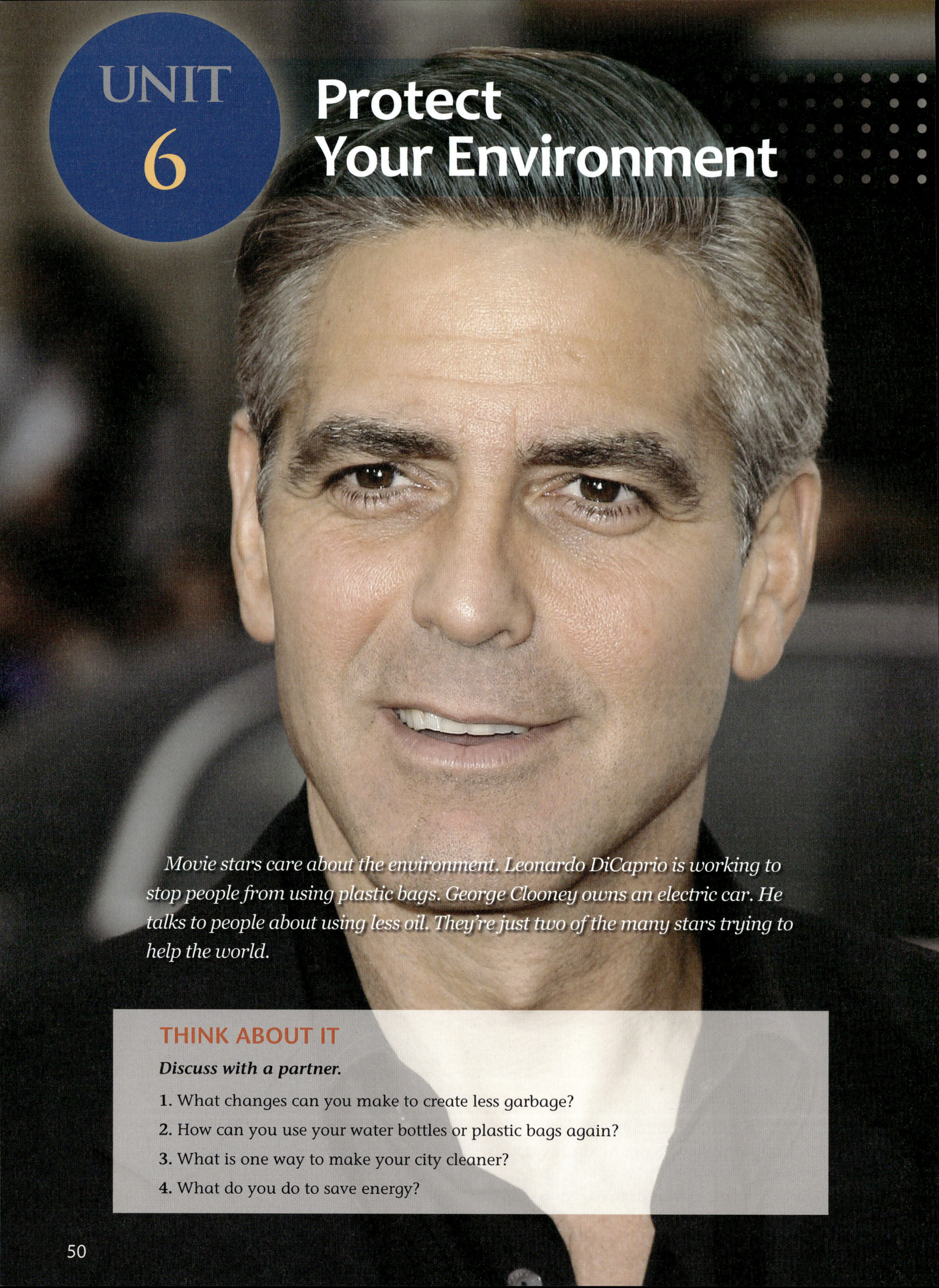

UNIT 6 Protect Your Environment

Movie stars care about the environment. Leonardo DiCaprio is working to stop people from using plastic bags. George Clooney owns an electric car. He talks to people about using less oil. They're just two of the many stars trying to help the world.

THINK ABOUT IT

Discuss with a partner.

1. What changes can you make to create less garbage?

2. How can you use your water bottles or plastic bags again?

3. What is one way to make your city cleaner?

4. What do you do to save energy?

Before We Read

A. Read and Answer

Answer the questions.

This quiz shows how ***environmentally friendly*** *you are. Circle your answer for each situation.*

1. When you brush your teeth, you ...
   a. turn off the water. b. leave the water running.
2. If you have old books or clothes you don't need, you ...
   a. **trade** with your family and friends. b. put them in the garbage can.
3. When you drink water, you ...
   a. **reuse** a cup and fill it with water. b. buy a plastic bottle of water.
4. If you go on vacation, you ...
   a. **unplug** unused **appliances**. b. keep appliances on.

If You Answer ...

Mostly a's You've done a good job in helping the environment. Well done!
Mostly b's You need to do more to keep the planet clean. Start with your everyday life!

Write the words in bold above in the appropriate space. Change the form of the words if necessary.

	Word	Definition
1		to pull a plug out of a socket
2		to use again
3		to give an item for something else
4		not damaging the environment
5		a machine that helps in the house

Use the words in bold above to complete the sentences. Change the form of the words if necessary.

1. I'll ________________ my chocolate for your ice cream.
2. Jim needs some ________________ for his new apartment.
3. Faith always ________________ her shopping bags.
4. Remember to ________________ your heater before going to sleep.
5. Plastic bags are not ________________.

B. Make Predictions

Read the title and the first paragraph on page 52. Answer the questions.

1. What does **green** mean in the article?
   - ☐ being new to a job
   - ☐ having a garden
   - ☐ helping the environment
   - ☐ wearing dark clothes
2. What will you probably read about next?
   - ☐ wearing nice clothes
   - ☐ ways to protect the earth
   - ☐ a creature from another planet
   - ☐ making money quickly

Now Let's Read

Go Green to Save the Planet

How can you save the planet and save money at the same time? Follow Cindy Crawford's "Easy, Green Tips for Everyday Life" to be more green.

1. Every year, over 38 billion plastic water bottles are thrown away. Stop buying extra bottles of water and reuse your water bottle.

2. Americans throw away almost 27 billion kilograms of food each year. Don't throw your food in the trash. Recycle it and use it in the garden.

3. Wash clothes in cold water. By doing this, you'll cut back on your energy bill.

4. Reuse plastic bags. Take your own bags with you whenever you go shopping.

5. Buy local food. Your food will be fresher. This also helps to keep the air clean because the food doesn't have to travel so far to reach your local supermarket.

6. Throw a green party. Ask your friends to come, so you can trade clothes with each other.

7. Unplug appliances that you don't use. This will help keep your energy bill low.

Comprehension Check

A. Fill in the Blanks

Complete the sentences with the words from the article.

1. You shouldn't ____________ water bottles in the garbage. You can reuse them.
2. Food that you don't eat can be ____________ and used in the garden.
3. If you wash your clothes in cold water, you will use less ____________.
4. ____________ food travels a shorter distance to the supermarket.
5. To be more green, you can ____________ clothes with your friends.
6. When you're not using ____________, like your computer or DVD player, you should ____________ them.

B. Make Inferences

What should we do to protect the earth? Check the answers.

- ☐ Disconnect your computer when you leave the house.
- ☐ Throw away all of the plastic water bottles that you use.
- ☐ Buy food that was grown close to your house.
- ☐ Wash clothes in warm water.
- ☐ Take your own bags with you when you go to the store.
- ☐ Use food you don't eat to grow things in a garden.

C. Multiple Choice

Circle the answer.

1. What can we say about Cindy Crawford?
   a. She isn't worried about the environment.
   b. She wants people to create less garbage.
   c. She is interested in saving money.
   d. She likes the color green.

2. Why should we wash our clothes in cold water?
   a. It will help us pay more money.
   b. It will help us wash our clothes faster.
   c. It will help us clean the clothes better.
   d. It will help us use less energy.

3. What kind of clothes can we trade with our friends?
   a. our favorite clothes
   b. our family's clothes
   c. clothes we don't need
   d. clothes we just bought

4. Which of the following is a reason to buy local food?
   a. It doesn't have to travel as far.
   b. It can be used again and again.
   c. It comes from farms in the mountains.
   d. It's grown in places far away from us.

5. Unplugging the machines in our house will ...
   a. keep the lights on longer.
   b. make our bills less expensive.
   c. save a lot of water.
   d. help us start recycling.

Vocabulary Check

A. Word Definitions

Match the word with its definition.

planet •	• power
energy •	• small; cheap
bill •	• a list showing how much you have to pay
low •	• a large, round object in space

B. Fill in the Blanks

*Use the words in bold from **A** to complete the sentences.*

1. I bought the computer because its price was ______________.
2. Wind power can be used to create ______________.
3. Scientists have found another ______________ just like the earth.
4. I pay my phone ______________ at the bank.

C. Words with Different Meanings

Match the word in bold with its definition.

1. Riding a bike is one way to **save** the planet. ______
   We will **save** a lot of time if we shop on the Internet. ______
   Definition: ⓐ *v.* to not waste ⓑ *v.* to make someone or something safe

2. Please **follow** me. I will take you to your table. ______
   Follow the doctor's advice and get more rest. ______
   Definition: ⓐ *v.* to do what someone says ⓑ *v.* to go after

3. The book gives many **tips** on cooking. ______
   I gave the waiter a $5 **tip**. ______
   Definition: ⓐ *n.* extra money you give ⓑ *n.* advice

4. Don't **throw** your clothes in the garbage. ______
   I'm going to **throw** a birthday party. ______
   Definition: ⓐ *v.* to put ⓑ *v.* to hold

D. Words in Context

Choose the answer.

1. I need to **cut back on** meat and eat more chicken / vegetables.
2. I always shop at **local** markets. All of the fruit is from farms that are close / far away.
3. The fruit is **fresh**. I just picked it from the garden / department store.
4. Dave ordered an **extra** hamburger. He was very dull / hungry.

Reading Strategy

Understanding Imperatives

TIP

When reading instructions, we will see imperatives. They are used to tell people what to do. The subject "you" is dropped and the sentence begins with a verb.

- **Don't eat** too much fast food.
- **Hand** in your assignment on time.

• Give It a Try •

PART I

Match the two columns.

Tips for Saving Water at Home

Take •	• faucets are turned off.
Turn off •	• when you have a full load.
Brush •	• fruit and vegetables in a pot.
Only wash clothes •	• the water while washing your face.
Wash •	• your teeth while waiting for the shower to get hot.
Make sure •	• shorter showers.

PART II

Complete the instructions with the word in the box.

get off	turn	walk	keep	take

A: Excuse me. How can I get to the train station?

B: ___________ bus 122. ___________ at City Park. Then, ___________ two blocks east and ___________ right. ___________ going until you see the train station.

PART III

Combine the verb and the rest part of the imperative. Write the sentences below.

Verb	The Rest of the Imperative
1. enter	the start button
2. put	your password
3. select	the piece of paper down here
4. push	the number of copies and paper size

First, ______________________________.

Then, ______________________________.

After that, ______________________________.

Finally, ______________________________.

Further Reading

Save the Planet in a Fun Way

Track 12

Saving the earth doesn't have to be very hard. Readers sent in ideas for environmental protection. These are our favorites:

No. 1 A Green Gym

You can go to the regular gym for your workout or try a green gym. These special gyms use machines that create energy. If people exercise fast enough, they can provide power for the gym's other machines and lights.

No. 2 An Eco-Nightclub*

Ready to dance? Want to help the environment also? A London nightclub has taken steps to be green. Its dance floor creates energy for the club's lights and music. Dancing here is one of the coolest ways to be green!

No. 3 This Idea Smells Good

A group in Nairobi had an eco-idea to make colorful glass art. They use gas that comes from animal (and human) waste to run the ovens that melt* glass. The group also uses only recycled materials to make their art, so it is both beautiful and green.

Recycling and turning off lights are a great start, but don't think saving the environment stops there. If you have a way to be eco-friendly, go for it!

Reference:

* **nightclub** *a place to dance and drink at night*
* **melt** *change something to liquid*

Comprehension Check

A. Classification

Match the sentence with the green idea from the passage. Write the number of the idea.

1. The exercise bikes can help keep the lights on. ______
2. All of the materials for our works of art have been recycled. ______
3. I want the music to keep playing. Let's keep dancing! ______
4. Running gives me energy, and now it's giving the gym energy too. ______
5. Being on a dance floor in London is a fun way to go green. ______
6. This is a great way to turn waste into something beautiful. ______

B. Topic Words

Use the words in the box to complete the sentences.

go green	eco-friendly	environmental protection

1. The president really cares about ______________.
2. Paper bags are more ______________ than plastic ones.
3. Walking to work is one way to ______________.

C. Words with Different Meanings

Match the word in bold with its definition.

a. to go fast	**b.** to manage	**c.** to operate

1. Only **run** the heater when it is really cold. ______
2. A dog **ran** out of the house. ______
3. The woman **ran** a coffee shop in Boston. ______

D. Multiple Choice

Circle the answer.

1. What is the reading mainly about?
   a. different ways to exercise
   b. new ideas for helping the earth
   c. how to use waste to create things
   d. where to have fun in London

2. What is special about the green gym?
   a. There are trees inside it.
   b. It uses the power of waste.
   c. Its machines make energy.
   d. It helps people get stronger.

3. Which of the following is closest to the meaning of **eco-**?
   a. healthy
   b. artistic
   c. beautiful
   d. environmental

4. What should people do if they have a new way to be eco-friendly?
   a. try hard to do it
   b. don't tell anybody
   c. spend more money for it
   d. go dancing

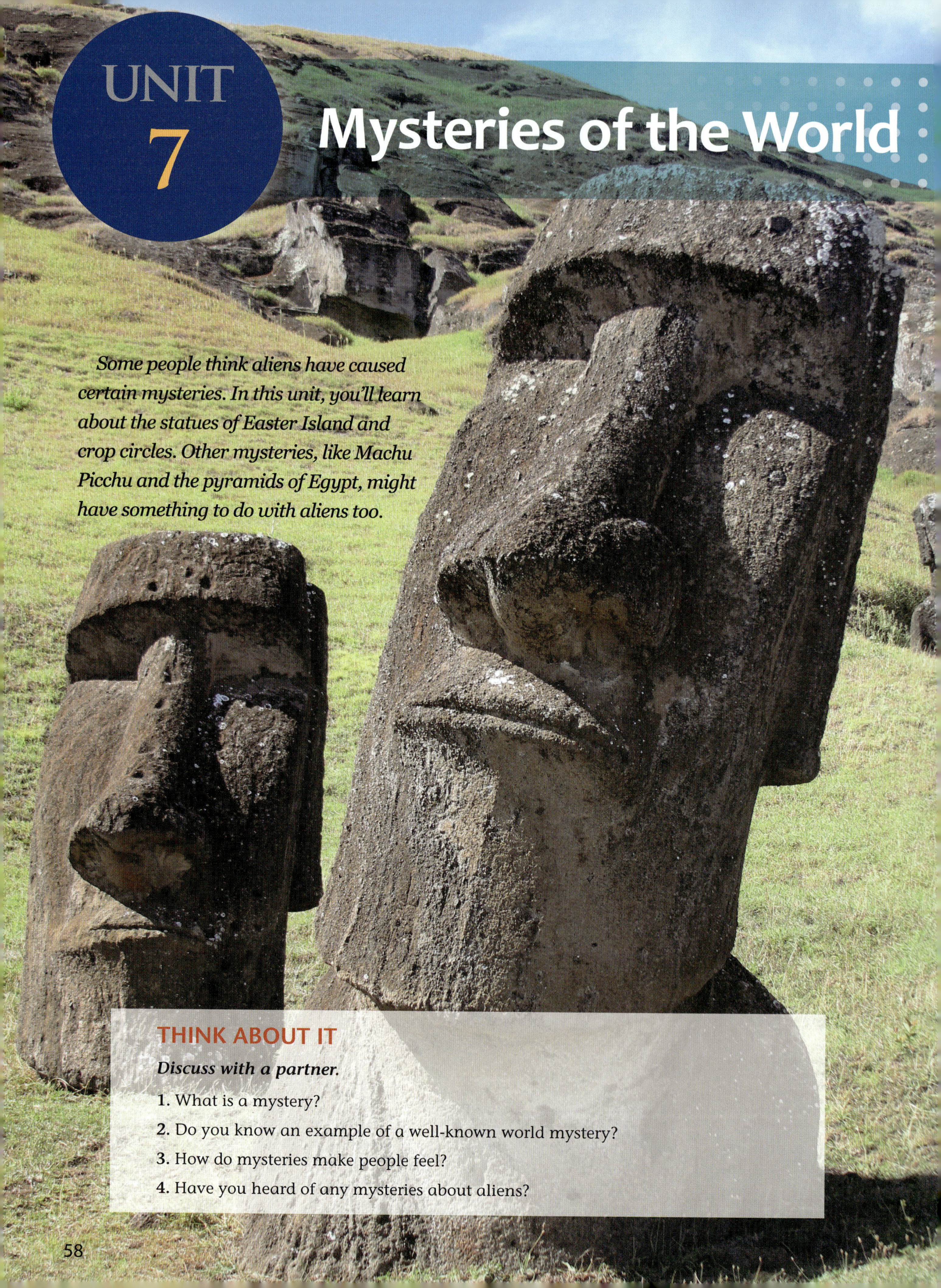

UNIT 7 Mysteries of the World

Some people think aliens have caused certain mysteries. In this unit, you'll learn about the statues of Easter Island and crop circles. Other mysteries, like Machu Picchu and the pyramids of Egypt, might have something to do with aliens too.

THINK ABOUT IT

Discuss with a partner.

1. What is a mystery?

2. Do you know an example of a well-known world mystery?

3. How do mysteries make people feel?

4. Have you heard of any mysteries about aliens?

Before We Read

A. Read and Answer

*Are you **curious** about these places? Read and make three questions about each picture. Then discuss them with your partner.*

The Bermuda **Triangle**, or the Devil's Triangle, is an area between Florida, Bermuda, and Puerto Rico.

These stone **statues** are called *moai*. They are seen all over Easter **Island**. A **giant** *moai* could be ten meters high.

Photo: Ian Sewell

Most circle designs are found in **fields** of **crops** in southern England. Some people think they are messages left by **aliens**.

Write the words in bold above in the appropriate space. Change the form of the words if necessary.

	Word	Definition
1		a shape with three sides
2		wanting to know about something
3		life from outer space
4		something made of stone or metal
5		land on a farm
6		land with water all around it
7		very big
8		a plant grown on a farm

Read the title and the first paragraph on page 60. What do you think the reading is about?

☐ strange people ☐ mysteries ☐ the world ☐ curiosity

B. Scan

Read the article on page 60. What do the following numbers refer to?

a. 200	**b.** 800	**c.** 250

1. crop circles that are made every year ______
2. head statues on Easter Island ______
3. the missing planes and ships in the Bermuda Triangle ______

Now Let's Read

Three Popular Mysteries

Many people are interested in mysteries. Strange places and things make us curious and also a little afraid. Have you heard about the following three mysteries?

Bermuda Triangle

Many planes and ships have disappeared in the Bermuda Triangle between Florida, Bermuda, and Puerto Rico. The most famous story was about Flight 19. A group of five aircraft became lost in the triangle and never came back. Some sources say more than 200 planes and ships have been reported missing.

Easter Island Statues

No one knows for certain who made or moved Easter Island's giant head statues. There are about 800 statues there. They are known for their large noses and strong chins. Some people believe they were made by the Inca of Peru. Others think aliens created **them**. Scientists say that Polynesians found the island, but the statues are still a mystery.

Crop Circles

Crop circles usually appear in farmers' fields. About 250 crop designs are created mysteriously around the world each year. In recent years, scientists have found that some are like DNA. Some people think the crop circles are made by aliens. In 1991, two Englishmen said they created the circles 15 years earlier. But they couldn't prove it. And people doubt they could make the designs in one night.

Comprehension Check

A. Short Answers

Write the answer.

1. Q: What was the Bermuda Triangle's most famous story about?

   A: ____

2. Q: What are Easter Island's stone head statues known for?

   A: ____

3. Q: Who do scientists say were the first people on Easter Island?

   A: ____

4. Q: In recent years, what have scientists found out about crop circles?

   A: ____

5. Q: When did the two Englishmen say they made the crop circles?

   A: ____

B. Classification

Match the sentence with the mystery.

a. Bermuda Triangle	b. Easter Island Statues	c. Crop Circles

1. These big stone heads are really strange. People think aliens made them. ______
2. Be careful when flying from Florida to Puerto Rico. A lot of planes have disappeared there. ______
3. What happened to this field? What are these big circles? ______
4. Wow! Look at the huge nose on that statue. ______
5. I don't think those two English guys could make such large designs in the field. ______
6. We never found pieces of the ship that disappeared. ______
7. The design in the crops looks like DNA. ______
8. Some people believe the Inca made the stone statues. ______

C. Multiple Choice

Circle the answer.

1. Where are crop circles usually found?

   a. fields
   b. islands
   c. ships
   d. Puerto Rico

2. Where is the Bermuda Triangle located?

   a. between England, Florida, and Bermuda
   b. between Peru, Bermuda, and Florida
   c. between Easter Island, Peru, and Puerto Rico
   d. between Puerto Rico, Florida, and Bermuda

3. Which of the stories in the article has aliens?

   a. Bermuda Triangle and Easter Island Statues
   b. Easter Island Statues and Crop Circles
   c. just Bermuda Triangle
   d. all of them

4. What does **them** refer to in the Easter Island Statues story?

   a. Polynesians
   b. aliens
   c. head statues
   d. the Inca people

Vocabulary Check

A. Word Definitions

Match the word with its definition.

aircraft •	• a person that gives you information
source •	• can't be found
missing •	• someone who works in science
chin •	• the part below your mouth
scientist •	• to show that something is true
prove •	• a plane, or a helicopter

B. Fill in the Blanks

*Use the words in bold from **A** to complete the sentences. Change the form of the words if necessary.*

1. The man looked around the town for his ______________ dog.
2. ______________ say that the earth is getting warmer based on the research.
3. The ______________ will arrive at the airport in 20 minutes.
4. It's difficult to ______________ that aliens are real.
5. A(n) ______________ told the newspaper that the president was going to resign.
6. Scott hurt his ______________ during a baseball game.

C. Antonyms

Match the word with its antonym.

strange •	• past
disappear •	• usual
recent •	• familiar
mysterious •	• appear

TIP

*The prefix **dis–** means "not," as in disappear. Can you guess what the antonyms of the following words are?*

- agree ↔ ______________ (not agree)
- like ↔ ______________ (not like)

D. Words with Different Meanings

Match the word in bold with its definition.

1
I **doubt** we will win. ______
There are some **doubts** about the safety of the building. ______
Definition: ⓐ *n.* feeling of not being sure ⓑ *v.* to think something may not happen

2
The aircraft was **reported** missing. ______
News **reports** said that three people were injured in the fire. ______
Definition: ⓐ *n.* a story of what happened ⓑ *v.* to tell someone what has happened

3
I **lost** my car keys. ______
I was **lost** in the forest. ______
Definition: ⓐ *adj.* not able to find the way ⓑ *v.* not to know where something is

Reading Strategy

Separating Facts from Opinions

TIP 1

A fact is something that can be proven. An opinion is someone's feeling about something.

TIP 2

Some clue words of opinions include:

I believe / feel / think ... In my opinion ... In my point of view ...
... is better / smarter than ... ... is the best / the greatest / the most beautiful ...

- **Fact:** Mount Everest is the highest mountain in the world.
- **Opinion:** I think Mount Everest is the most amazing mountain in the world.

• Give It a Try •

PART I

*Check **Fact** or **Opinion**.*

		Fact	Opinion
1.	People shouldn't be interested in mysteries.	☐	☐
2.	Planes and ships have disappeared in the Bermuda Triangle.	☐	☐
3.	Easter Island's giant head statues have large noses and strong chins.	☐	☐
4.	There are about 800 head statues on Easter Island.	☐	☐
5.	The head statues on Easter Island were probably made by the Inca of Peru.	☐	☐
6.	Crop circles usually appear in fields of crops.	☐	☐
7.	Scientists found that some crop circles are like DNA.	☐	☐
8.	I think crop circles may be the work of aliens.	☐	☐

PART II

Underline the sentences that are opinions.

Some mysterious stories in the world get a lot of attention. However, I don't believe in most of them. Take Area 51 for example. Area 51 is the name of a U.S. military base in Nevada. The American government says it uses the base to test new aircraft. Some people think aliens have landed near Area 51. They also believe that the U.S. has studied aliens there. In my point of view, it's just a place to test new airplanes and weapons.

View from above Area 51
Photo: United States Geological Survey

A Mystery Tour of Britain

Track 14

This book will take you across Britain to learn about everything from lake monsters to a group of large stones. Come along on a trip to some of the country's most mysterious places.

Start at a circle of large rocks in a field. This is Stonehenge. Some scientists say part of it was built around 3000 B.C. with stones from far away. Find out people's opinions about why Stonehenge was made.

Next, the book takes you west to Somerset, where the Wookey Hole Caves are. People say the caves were once home to a witch.* One day, a priest was sent to cure the Wookey Hole Witch. When the witch tried to run away, she was turned to stone. The stone is still inside the caves.

The book's last stop is up north in Loch Ness, Scotland. This is where people have seen the famous Loch Ness Monster. The monster has a long neck. Some say they have seen the giant animal swimming in the lake. However, no one has **proof** yet.

Take the book with you on your visit to Britain. You are sure to have an exciting, mysterious trip.

Reference:

* **witch** *a woman with special powers*

Comprehension Check

A. Word Usage

*Do you know the difference between **tour**, **visit**, and **trip**?*

- Thousands of people **visit** her blog every day.
- Come along on a **trip** / **visit** to some of the country's most mysterious places.
- We saw many lions during our **tour** of the animal park yesterday.

Use the words in bold above to complete the sentences. Change the form of the words if necessary. More than one answer is possible.

1. It's a beautiful day. We should go on a fishing ______________.
2. Thousands of people ______________ Hong Kong every year.
3. The travel company took us on a ten-day ______________ of America last month.
4. We are ______________ France for our summer vacation this year.

B. True or False

*Check **True** or **False**.*

	True	False
1. Stonehenge is a large castle in a field.	☐	☐
2. No one knows for sure that the Loch Ness Monster is real.	☐	☐
3. You can go to Somerset, England to find the Wookey Hole Caves.	☐	☐
4. Some say the stones of Stonehenge come from a distance.	☐	☐
5. The maps in the book are difficult to read.	☐	☐

C. Multiple Choice

Circle the answer.

1. What type of reading is this?
   a. an email
   b. a book summary
   c. a children's story
   d. a postcard

2. What can we say about Stonehenge?
   a. It was built a short time ago.
   b. It is in the middle of a lake.
   c. The stones were made by a priest.
   d. It is east of the Wookey Hole Caves.

3. Where did the witch live?
   a. in the cave
   b. in a church
   c. Loch Ness, Scotland
   d. in a lake

4. According to people, the Loch Ness Monster ...
   a. has a very short neck.
   b. hasn't been seen by people.
   c. lives in a lake in Scotland.
   d. doesn't swim at all.

5. What does **proof** mean in the fourth paragraph?
   a. the history of a lake in Scotland
   b. an old song passed down through the generation
   c. information proving something is true
   d. a map of Loch Ness, Scotland

UNIT 8

Gap Years

THINK ABOUT IT

Discuss with a partner.

1. Do you think it's a good idea to take a year off school?

2. If you take a year off, what would you like to do?

3. Who do you think need a gap year?

Before We Read

A. Read and Answer

*A gap year is when you take time **off** from school to travel. Let's see if the idea is good for you.*

1. When making **decisions**, I usually ...
   - **a.** decide right away.
   - **b.** think for a while.
   - **c.** don't like deciding anything.

2. In my lifetime, I have **traveled** ...
   - **a.** to many countries.
   - **b.** to a few countries with my parents.
   - **c.** to no countries at all.

3. While at school, I have ...
   - **a.** had lots of job **experiences**.
   - **b.** had a few job experiences.
   - **c.** never had any job experiences.

4. During my teenage years, I have ...
   - **a.** done **volunteer** work at home and **overseas**.
   - **b.** done some volunteer work but not a lot.
   - **c.** never done volunteer work.

5. My parents usually ...
   - **a.** let me do what I want.
   - **b.** give me some space.
   - **c.** tell me what to do.

6. I ________ what I want to do in the future.
   - **a.** know
   - **b.** am thinking about
   - **c.** don't know

Scoring

a. 3 points
b. 2 points
c. 1 point

Results

15 to 18	You don't need a gap year. You have a clear idea of what to do with your future.
9 to 14	You might need a gap year. A year off will help you decide what you want to do.
6 to 8	A gap year would probably help. You don't seem to know what you want.

Write the words in bold above in the appropriate space. Change the form of the words if necessary.

	Word	Definition
1		not paid for doing a job
2		a choice you make
3		to go from one place to another
4		being in a foreign country
5		something you learn from doing an activity
6		not at school or work

B. Make Predictions

Read the title on page 68. What do you think the reading is about?

- ☐ young people trying something new
- ☐ someone trying to buy a real watch
- ☐ a gap in the ages of the children
- ☐ traveling all over the world

Now Let's Read

Experiencing the Real World

Track 15

In some countries, many students don't go to college right after they finish high school. Instead they take a year off before starting college. This is called a gap year. Some students use the time to travel overseas. Others get a job and earn money. Some students choose to do volunteer work.

Emma Watson took a gap year before attending Brown University. She used the time to work with fair trade fashion brand *People Tree* designing T-shirts, dresses, and skirts for teens. Prince Harry spent his gap year in a variety of experiences: he spent three months working on a ranch in Australia. He also worked in Lesotho, building a clinic and a bridge, and visited an orphanage for children with AIDS.

Some parents don't want their kids to take a gap year. They want their kids to continue their studies. They think that their children will forget their lessons from high school. They believe that it's best for their children to finish education first. Other parents love the gap year idea. They want their kids to see the real world and become more independent. Parents argue that this experience will help **their** kids make better decisions.

Taking a gap year is becoming more common around the world. Someday, maybe everyone will take a year off. After all, not all knowledge is found in books.

Comprehension Check

A. Complete the Chart

Fill in the blanks with the words from the article. Change the form of the words if necessary.

What Do Parents Think about Gap Years?

Like	• Parents hope their children can travel and become more ____________.
	• Parents believe that this ____________ will help their children in the future.
Dislike	• Parents think that their children will ____________ what they have learned in high school.
	• Parents argue that it's better for students to finish their ____________ as soon as possible.

B. True or False

*Check **True** or **False**.*

		True	False
1.	Every student goes to the college right after high school.	☐	☐
2.	Nobody makes money during a gap year.	☐	☐
3.	Some parents believe a gap year is good for their children.	☐	☐
4.	Taking a gap year is less common now.	☐	☐
5.	Some parents think a gap year will help their children understand the real world.	☐	☐
6.	Even celebrities take a gap year for new experience.	☐	☐
7.	People who take a gap year always want to earn money.	☐	☐

C. Multiple Choice

Circle the answer.

1. What do students NOT do during their gap year?

a. get a job
b. try volunteer work
c. attend college
d. go traveling

2. What did Emma Watson do during her gap year?

a. travel around Australia
b. care for orphans
c. work in the fashion field
d. build a bridge

3. What does **their** refer to in the third paragraph?

a. parents
b. kids
c. children
d. lessons

4. The writer thinks taking a gap year ...

a. is becoming more popular.
b. is not a very good idea.
c. is a waste of time.
d. is too expensive.

Vocabulary Check

A. Complete the Sentences

Fill in the blanks with the words in the box. Change the form of the words if necessary.

experience	travel	work	take

1. I have some ______________ in teaching English.
2. Let's go for a drink after ______________.
3. Sarah will ______________ a year off after this semester.
4. I want to study overseas and ______________ different cultures.
5. We ______________ across China by train last summer.
6. My grandfather ______________ for a restaurant before.
7. Taking a bus is cheaper than air ______________.
8. It ______________ time to learn a new language.

B. Fill in the Missing Letters

Complete the sentences with the words from the article.

1. James will **c**____________ to play on this basketball team next fall.
2. He **e**____________ more than $20,000 a year.
3. Tom is working as a **v**____________ at an orphanage every weekend.
4. **C**____________ under 12 can't watch this movie.
5. Edwin hopes his son will get a good **e**____________ at the best school.
6. Lily often travels **o**____________. She had been to more than 20 countries.
7. He doesn't have any background **k**____________ to do this job.
8. Carrie studied English at a well-known **c**____________.

C. Meanings in Context

Choose the meaning of the sentence.

1. I called Nick **right after** I got home.
   a. I called Nick before I got home.
   b. I called Nick as soon as I got home.

2. Mandy has to **take** one day **off** because she is sick.
   a. Mandy is still coming to work.
   b. Mandy isn't coming to work.

3. Diana is an **independent** young woman. She can do this by herself.
   a. Diana is able to do things on her own.
   b. Diana often asks for help.

4. The writer **argues** that war is bad.
   a. The writer doesn't accept war.
   b. The writer has a positive opinion about war.

Reading Strategy

Comparing and Contrasting

Circle the words that show comparing and contrasting. Then fill in the chart.

In Korea, students usually go to college right after high school. In other countries, students also choose to continue. However, they often take a year off before starting college.

Students in Korea and Students in Other Countries

How They Are Alike	How They Are Different
go to college right after high school	take a year off before starting college

• Give It a Try •

PART I

Doug lives in Canada. He just graduated, but he will take a gap year before working. He will choose one of the programs below.

Train for the Marathon

- Lose weight
- Do something difficult
- Eat my mom's delicious home cooking
- Save a lot of money by not taking a trip
- Have time to think about the future

Travel to India

- See the Taj Mahal
- Learn about a new culture
- Visit a beautiful country
- Eat delicious Indian food every day
- Think about what I want to do in the future

PART II

Fill in the blanks with the words in the box.

although	or	as well	however	both

1. Doug can stay in Canada ______________ go to India.
2. He really wants to learn about a new culture in India. ______________, going to India costs a lot of money.
3. He can think about the future if he trains for the marathon. He can do so if he goes to India ______________.
4. He can eat well in ______________ Canada and India.
5. ______________ going to India is expensive, he can see a beautiful country.

Further Reading

Thinking About Taking a Year Off?

Track 16

More and more people are taking gap years. We sat down with three people to ask why.

Nicole Wheels, London, England

I have lots of interesting ideas in my head. But I used to be too shy to share. So, I went to Los Angeles to take acting classes. I'll never forget my first play. My body was shaking. When I went on the stage, however, I calmed down and did well. I'm still shy, but now I can control it. Sometimes, I even give my phone number to handsome guys.

Susan Wang, Ottawa, Canada

I think living in Kenya changed me. I realized there that money isn't the most important thing. We showed people how to work on a modern farm. We gave them knowledge. This is a gift that is forever. It felt good helping others. Going to Kenya gave me something too — experience. I hope to go back someday.

Mike Carson, Berkeley, California

I studied Chinese in college, but I never had a chance to practice. All my friends spoke English, even my Chinese friends. So, I decided to go to China between my first and second year. After six months, my Chinese had improved a lot. I could talk about food, weather, and the news. I still made mistakes, but people understood me. If you're interested in learning a language, put yourself in the right environment. It's the best and most interesting way to improve.

Comprehension Check

A. Complete the Chart

Fill in the chart with the words from the article.

	Nicole	Susan	Mike
Countries they visited			
Things they did			
Things they learned			

B. Antonyms

Write the antonyms of the following words/phrases from the article.

	Word/Phrase	Antonym		Word/Phrase	Antonym
1	boring		2	old-fashioned	
3	confident		4	temporary	
5	get nervous		6	get worse	

C. Fill in the Blanks

*Use the words from **B** to complete the sentences.*

1. This book is very ______________. I can't put it down.
2. Luke doesn't like talking that much. He's very ______________.
3. Don't give the kids too much sugar. If you do, they'll never ______________.
4. That building is so ______________. I've never seen anything like it before.

D. Multiple Choice

Circle the answer.

1. What is the reading mainly about?
   a. People take gap years for different reasons.
   b. Acting classes can help someone speak better.
   c. Working on a farm make someone earn lots of money.
   d. When people take gap years, they get gifts.

2. What happened to Nicole the first time she got on the stage?
   a. She did a bad job.
   b. Her face got red.
   c. She became relaxed and did well.
   d. She became much shyer and didn't move at all.

3. What did Susan teach people in Kenya?
   a. how to help others
   b. the importance of money
   c. a new language
   d. new ways to plant things

4. Why did Mike go to China?
   a. to meet Chinese friends
   b. to speak Chinese better
   c. to teach English
   d. to go on vacation

UNIT 9 Get Rich Quick

THINK ABOUT IT

Discuss with a partner.

1. Have you ever bought a lottery ticket?
2. What would you do if you won the lottery?
3. How long do you think people have been playing the lottery?
4. What's the largest lottery prize you have ever heard of?

Before We Read

A. Read and Answer

How do most lottery winners ***spend*** *their* ***winnings****? Match the sentence parts.*

Put •	• poor people.
Share •	• **debts.**
Buy •	• money with family or friends.
Pay off •	• a vacation.
Take •	• a new house.
Help •	• money in the bank.

Write the words/phrases in bold above in the appropriate space. Change the form of the words if necessary.

	Word/Phrase	Definition
1		to pay back the money
2		to use your money to pay for something
3		money you have won
4		money you have borrowed

B. Make Predictions

Read the top part of the article on page 76. Answer the questions.

1. Where does the text come from?

☐ a novel
☐ an advertisement
☐ a magazine
☐ a travel blog

2. What do you think the reading is about?

☐ traveling in different countries
☐ plans for starting a business
☐ necessity of saving money
☐ a nice product for cleaning the floor
☐ ideas on winning a prize
☐ a family member

C. Scan

Read the article on page 76. Answer the questions.

1. When could people first read the story?
2. What is the second thing he would do if he won the lottery?
3. Would he be a good landlord?
4. What would he buy for his family and friends?
5. What would he get for himself?

Q&A What Would I Do if I Won the Lottery?

Track 17

Share with Annie

Dear Annie,

First, if I won the lottery, I wouldn't tell a lot of people.

Second, I would buy some houses and rent them out. If I had tenants, I would have a regular income. I would be a good landlord and make sure everything was clean and worked well. I would treat all of my tenants the same. Everyone would say I was fair.

Next, I'd use some of the money to help poor people. Of course, I would also help out my family and good friends. I'd buy them lots of nice things.

Lastly, I would spend some money on myself. I would buy a notebook computer, computer games, and expensive food. I would also take part in interesting classes.

Best,
Jeff

Dear Jeff,

Thank you for your letter. I like your ideas. You said that you would not tell everyone if you won the lottery. That is a smart idea. Your plan for what to do with your winnings is noteworthy. Many people only think about spending money. However, you thought about a way to earn money in the future, too. You also planned to help other people. I admire you.

All in all, I respect your ideas.

Sincerely,
Annie

Comprehension Check

A. Complete the Sentences

Fill in the blanks with the words in the box. Change the form of the words if necessary.

poor	tenant	take part in	plan	landlord

1. If I had ______________, I would be able to get a regular income every month.
2. I would be a good ______________ and make sure everything was clean and worked well.
3. I'd like to use some of the money to help ______________ people.
4. I want to ______________ interesting classes for myself.
5. I really liked your ______________ for what to do with your winnings.

B. Make Inferences

Match the sentence with its inference.

a. Jeff likes to eat.	**b.** Jeff cares about people without money.
c. Jeff is careful with his money.	**d.** Jeff enjoys learning something new.

1. I would use some of the money to help poor people. ______
2. I would buy some expensive food. ______
3. I would also take part in interesting classes. ______
4. You thought about a way to earn money in the future. ______

C. Multiple Choice

Circle the answer.

1. If Jeff won the lottery, he would NOT ...
   a. buy houses.
   b. help the poor.
   c. spend money for his family.
   d. give classes to children.

2. Which of the following is true?
   a. Jeff only cares about poor people.
   b. Jeff wants to sell the houses he owns.
   c. Jeff will spend some of the money on himself.
   d. Jeff won't help anyone except his good friends.

3. Why does Annie like Jeff's letter?
   a. She thinks he has some good ideas.
   b. His letter is neat.
   c. She thinks they can become friends.
   d. He tells her how to win a lottery.

4. What does **all in all** mean in the second letter?
   a. completely
   b. in general
   c. kind of
   d. not at all

Vocabulary Check

A. Words with Different Meanings

Match the word in bold with its definition.

1. Most students **rent** houses near the school. _____
   I pay the **rent** at the end of every month. _____
   Definition: ⓐ *v.* to pay money to live in a house ⓑ *n.* monthly house payment

2. Could you give me more **clean** towels? _____
   My mother **cleans** the kitchen every day. _____
   Definition: ⓐ *n.* to change something that is dirty ⓑ *adj.* free from dirt

3. Ms. Thompson believes all of the students are the same. She is very **fair**. _____
   You can find lots of cheap books at the book **fair**. _____
   Definition: ⓐ *n.* an event at which people sell something ⓑ *adj.* thinking everyone is equal

B. Meanings in Context

Choose the meaning of the sentence.

1. Iris is making dinner. Let's **help** her **out**.
   a. Let's do it together.
   b. Iris will do it by herself.

2. Mike will **take part in** our surfing class.
   a. Mike will join our surfing class.
   b. Mike will not come to our surfing class.

3. **In the future**, people will work less every week.
   a. People worked less before.
   b. People will work less later.

C. Word Definitions

Match the word with its definition.

regular •	• someone who rents a house to people
income •	• someone who rents a house from another person
tenant •	• money that you get from your work
landlord •	• happening every hour, week, or month

D. Complete the Passage

Fill in the blanks with the words in bold from **C**.

Jack likes being a __________. If there's a problem, he calls his __________, Mr. Brown. Mr. Brown is a __________ visitor too. He comes to Jack's apartment once a week. All in all, Jack is happy renting an apartment. He has a good __________, so he can always pay the rent.

Reading Strategy

Listing Things in Order

TIP

When we talk about actions or events that happen one after another, we usually use the following words:

first	first of all	then
second	after	next
third	after that	finally / lastly

- It's easy to make! Just follow a few steps. **First**, open the can and put what's inside into a pan. **Then**, add one cup of water. **Next**, put the pan on the fire. **When** your food is hot, cook it for three minutes. **Finally**, serve it in a bowl. Can you guess what it is? It's soup. It's so simple that anyone could make it.

• Give It a Try •

PART I

Fill in the blanks with the words in the box.

then	7:15	while	after	finally	first	six a.m.

I usually get up at ______________, and I always do the same thing. ______________, I drink a cup of coffee. If I don't drink coffee, I'll feel tired. ______________ I'm drinking coffee, I read the newspaper. ______________ that, I make breakfast for my family and my cat. ______________, I take a shower and get ready for work. ______________, I leave the house. If I leave later than ______________, I'll be late. How about you? How do you start your day?

PART II

Put the following events in order.

a. Our office is the glass building next to the post office.
b. To get to our office, follow these directions.
c. Then walk straight for two blocks, until you come to Broadway.
d. Turn right on Broadway.
e. After that, walk down Broadway for five minutes.
f. When you get off the subway, leave the station from exit six.
g. First, take the subway to 5th Road station.

_____ → _____ → _____ → _____ → _____ → _____ → _____

Further Reading

A Game of Chance

Track 18

Are you feeling lucky? Maybe it's time to buy a lottery ticket. The lottery has been around for thousands of years and it is still a popular game today.

Early Lotteries

Some of the first lotteries were held in China during the Han Dynasty. Back then, the government used lottery money to build things like the Great Wall. At around the same time, the lottery was becoming popular in Europe. It was a fun and interesting type of game to play at dinner parties. Caesar also used a lottery to help pay for repairs in Rome.

The Game Spreads

The lottery became popular in Europe again in the 1500s. In Belgium, lottery money was used to build houses for the poor. Queen Elizabeth ran the lottery in England and gave away prizes like silverware.* In the 1700s, lottery money helped build the British Museum.

Photo: Free Software Foundation

Moving to America

England also used lottery money to start building towns in America. During the Revolutionary War, Benjamin Franklin held a lottery to buy guns for the army. After the war ended, lotteries were used to build churches, hospitals, and libraries. Even famous schools like Yale, Harvard, and Princeton were built with money from the lottery!

Today, lotteries are played by people all over the world. The largest lottery prize ever given out to one person was $182 million. It's no wonder people love to play the lottery.

Reference:

* **silverware** *knives, forks, and spoons that are made of silver*

Comprehension Check

A. Details

How was lottery money used in the past? Check the answers.

☐ to hold dinner parties	☐ to repair Rome	☐ to help the poor
☐ to make a museum	☐ to pay for a ship	☐ to build towns in Canada
☐ to get guns for soldiers	☐ to make walls in England	☐ to build schools and churches

B. True or False

*Check **True** or **False**.*

	True	False
1. The lottery is a new and popular game.	☐	☐
2. The Chinese government used lottery money to buy buildings.	☐	☐
3. Yale, Harvard, and Princeton were all built with lottery money.	☐	☐
4. America helped build towns in England with lottery money.	☐	☐
5. The largest lottery prize in history was close to $200 million.	☐	☐

C. Fill in the Blanks

Complete the sentences with the words in parentheses. Change the form of the words if necessary.

1. He ______________ (use) all of his money to buy paintings.
2. Meetings will be ______________ (hold) every Monday morning.
3. The games ______________ (run) when the students finished class.
4. The wedding industry is ______________ (become) bigger and bigger these days.

D. Multiple Choice

Circle the answer.

1. What is the reading mainly about?
   a. how to play and win the lottery
   b. different types of lottery prizes
   c. the history of the lottery
   d. people who play the lottery

2. What is another appropriate title for the article?
   a. Playing to Win!
   b. The Lottery — Past and Present
   c. Lotteries for the Poor
   d. Fun Party Games

3. How was the lottery used in Belgium?
   a. It was used to help people who didn't have money.
   b. It was used to build a new house for the queen.
   c. It was used to buy silverware and other things.
   d. It was used to get guns and money for a war.

UNIT 10 Foods That Make You Happy

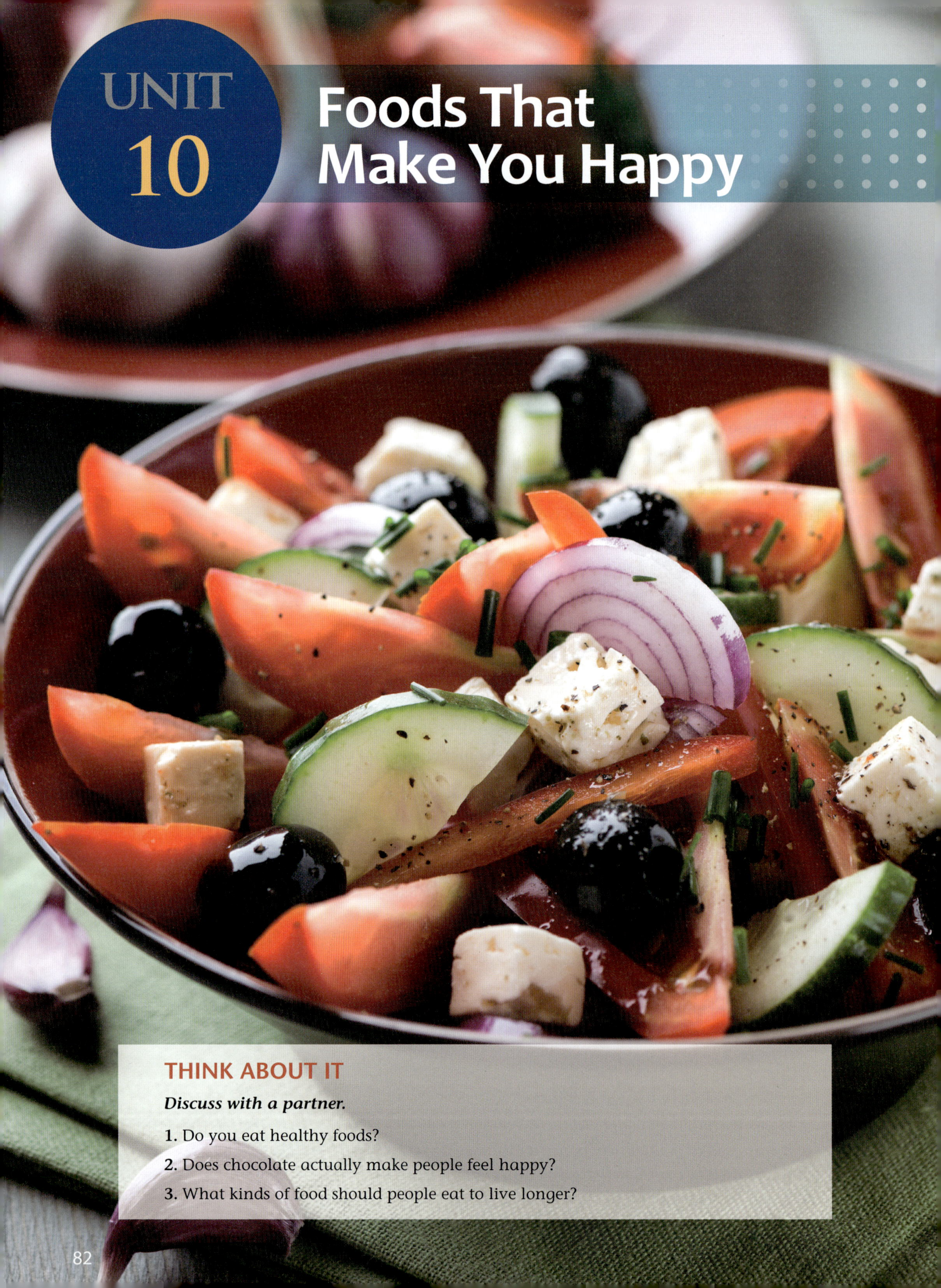

THINK ABOUT IT

Discuss with a partner.

1. Do you eat healthy foods?

2. Does chocolate actually make people feel happy?

3. What kinds of food should people eat to live longer?

Before We Read

A. Read and Answer

Eat Fish, Be Healthy

Oily fish, like salmon or sardines, are rich in omega-3 **fatty** acids. One study in Finland shows that people who eat more fish are less likely to have **depression**. These fish oils are good for your heart and brain **as well**.

Scientists Say ...

- Eating oily fish can help you avoid heart problems.
- **Vitamin** D in oily fish builds teeth and bones.
- Omega-3 fatty acids may **improve** your learning skills.

Write the words in bold above in the appropriate space.

	Word	Definition
1		not feeling happy
2		too; also
3		to make something better
4		oily; having a lot of oil
5		a substance that is good for your health

Use the words in bold above to complete the sentences. Change the form of the words if necessary.

1. Eat well and exercise regularly to avoid ______________.
2. James doesn't eat fried chicken because he thinks it's too ______________.
3. After Sue moved to America, her English ______________ a lot.
4. Don likes to play basketball. Chris does ______________.
5. Nick is too weak and thin. He has to take ______________ to stay healthy.

B. Make Predictions

Read the title on page 84. What do you think the reading is about?

☐ how foods influence us
☐ some foods taste better
☐ trying to eat more food
☐ being smart in school

Now Let's Read

Eat Well, Eat Smart

Track 19

Everyone knows that delicious food makes people happy, but science shows that some foods make you happier than others. For example, foods with omega-3 fatty acids, like fish and beans, can help you think faster. Knowing the answers and doing well on tests makes us all feel good.

Studies tell us that eating more omega-3 foods has other positive effects. It helps to stop heart problems, depression, and even crime! When scientists gave vitamins and omega-3 fatty acids to people in a British prison, violence dropped 37 percent.

Eat whole grain foods like brown rice and whole wheat bread if you feel depressed. Whole grains can also make you happier because they help your brain make serotonin,* which keeps you calm. Scientists say that people with low levels of serotonin feel angry and fight more often.

Eating chocolate and drinking coffee can improve your mood as well, but that's no surprise. They both cause the brain to give off endorphins* — the body's natural medicine. Be careful about drinking too much coffee though. This can make you nervous and unable to sleep.

The food you eat can change the way you feel. Eat these foods every day and you'll be both happy and healthy.

Reference:

* **serotonin** *a chemical produced naturally in the brain that makes people feel better*
* **endorphin** *a group of peptide hormones occurring naturally in the brain that take away pain*

Comprehension Check

A. True or False

Check ***True*** *or* ***False.***

	True	False
1. Foods such as fish and beans are good for your brain.	☐	☐
2. Studies tell us that omega-3 foods cause more heart problems.	☐	☐
3. Whole grains help you keep calm.	☐	☐
4. Whole grains are foods like chocolate and coffee.	☐	☐
5. The more you drink coffee, the better you feel.	☐	☐
6. Eating chocolate can make you happy.	☐	☐

B. Details

Write the number of the paragraph to match each detail.

1. You won't be able to sleep if you drink too much coffee. _____
2. Fish and beans help you think faster and therefore feel happy. _____
3. Scientists gave omega-3 foods to people in a British prison. _____
4. People with high levels of serotonin usually don't feel angry. _____
5. People who eat whole grain foods seldom fight. _____
6. Eating omega-3 foods helps us stop depression and crime. _____
7. Omega-3 fatty acids give us a strong heart. _____
8. Chocolate and coffee help you get endorphins. _____
9. Brown rice and whole wheat bread are two kinds of whole grains. _____

C. Multiple Choice

Circle the answer.

1. Which of the following is true?
   a. Any food can make us happier.
   b. Fish and beans make us sleepy.
   c. Foods influence us differently.
   d. Taking tests makes us feel good.

2. Getting more omega-3 foods helps with all of these problems BUT ...
   a. sadness.
   b. robbery.
   c. health.
   d. money.

3. Whole grains make serotonin in our brain ...
   a. which keeps us calm.
   b. which lowers serotonin.
   c. which makes us feel angry.
   d. which makes us want to fight.

4. We need to avoid having too ____________ for deep sleep.
   a. many whole grains
   b. much coffee
   c. much brown rice
   d. much fish

Vocabulary Check

A. Antonyms

Match the word with its antonym.

fatty •	• **nervous**
smart •	• **depressed**
positive •	• **low-fat**
calm •	• able
happy •	• foolish
unable •	• negative

B. Fill in the Blanks

*Use the words in bold from **A** to complete the sentences.*

1. Don't give up. You need to be more ______________.
2. I usually eat ______________ foods. I know they're good for my health.
3. Whenever it is raining, Janet is ______________ and feels like crying.
4. I'm not worried about the test. I'm very ______________.
5. Sorry, but I'm ______________ to speak Chinese. Could you please speak in English?
6. Everyone feels ______________ when they have to give a speech.

C. Words in Context

Choose the answer.

1. The news has a bad **effect** on me. It influences / helps me.
2. **Crime** often happens in a big city. There are a lot of friendly / bad people there.
3. Dylan was put in **prison** because he did something right / wrong.
4. There is too much **violence** on TV. People always hit / hug each other.
5. I wanted to eat some **whole grains**, so I bought brown rice / tomatoes.
6. The weather changes Tara's **mood**. It makes her smell / feel different.

D. Complete the Sentences

Fill in the blanks with the words in the box. Some blanks have more than one answer.

also	too	as well	either

1. Pam likes to shop. Her sister ______________ likes to shop.
2. Barry doesn't like seafood, and I don't ______________.
3. Pedro has been to Mexico. I have ______________.
4. Please give me a hamburger and fries. I want some ice cream ______________.

TIP

Too *and* ***also*** *are both used to agree.* ***Too*** *is often placed at the end of a sentence.* ***Either*** *is used to end negative sentences.*

Reading Strategy

Understanding Cause and Effect

TIP

We usually use the following words to introduce cause and effect.

Cause:

because	the reason for	because of	since	as

Effect:

so	as a result	therefore	for this reason	thus

- We didn't enjoy the restaurant **because** the food was bad.
- I was feeling tired; **therefore**, I went to bed.
- **Because of** the weather, we couldn't go to the beach.

• Give It a Try •

PART I

Match the cause and effect.

Effect

a. Violence dropped 37 percent.
b. You'll start to get nervous and have trouble sleeping.
c. They can make you feel less nervous.
d. Omega-3 foods will make us smart.

Cause

1. Our brain must have omega-3 fatty acids to work well. ______
2. People in a prison in Britain had vitamins and omega-3 fatty acids. ______
3. Whole grains help you make a special chemical to feel calm. ______
4. Drink many cups of coffee every day. ______

PART II

Combine the two sentences with the word in parentheses.

1. There is too much pollution. / People can't breathe and have health problems. (because)
   → ______________________________
2. People have cut down too many trees. / There is more carbon dioxide(CO^2). (so)
   → ______________________________
3. The sea level is rising. / Many small islands are disappearing. (therefore)
   → ______________________________

Further Reading

Okinawa : The Secret to Long Life

Track 20

Over the past 100 years, **life expectancy** has increased by 30 years. Today, people in 61 countries live more than 75 years. Okinawa, a group of Japanese islands, leads the way. Okinawan women live to be 86 years old. Men, on the other hand, live until 78.

So, what's their secret to long life? First, people in Okinawa eat healthy foods. They don't eat fatty hamburgers or fries; they prefer vegetables and soy foods. Studies show that Okinawans get seven servings* of fruit and vegetables every day and sometimes even more! They don't often have red meat or dairy* products, such as milk or cheese. And they eat three or fewer sweet foods a day.

Experts say the custom of hara hachi bu, which means "only eat until you're 80 percent full," is also important. Eating too much can really hurt our bodies. In the West, all-you-can-eat restaurants are popular. But there aren't many of these places in Okinawa. People there seldom eat more than they need.

Okinawa has a population of one million and there are 900 people over the age of 100. That's four times better than the Western rate.* Do you want to live to be 100? If the answer is yes, take a look at these islands.

Reference:

- * **serving** *an amount of food for one person*
- * **dairy** *a place where milk is kept and butter or cheese is made*
- * **rate** *a percent*

Comprehension Check

Extra Info

Look at the chart. Make comparatives with a partner.

Country	Life Expectancy for Women	Life Expectancy for Men
Iceland	83.3	80.2
Australia	84.4	77.7
Vietnam	76.6	72.2
Liberia	40.4	39.7
Zambia	40.4	40.1
Swaziland	39.8	39.4

- Women in Liberia live as long as women in Zambia.
- Men in Australia live longer than men in Vietnam.

A. Details

Which of the following pictures is more like the diet of an Okinawan? Choose the answers.

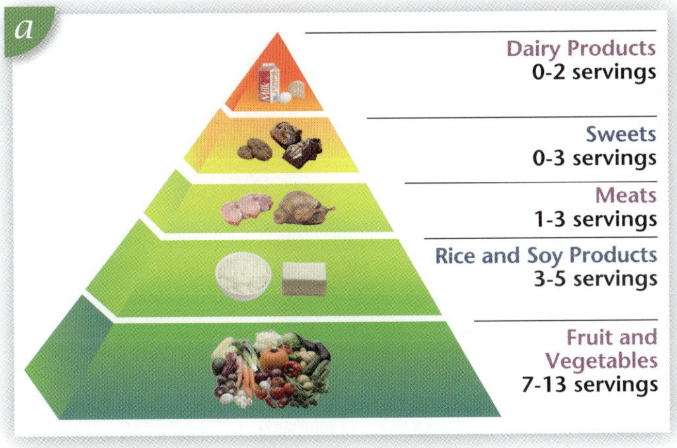

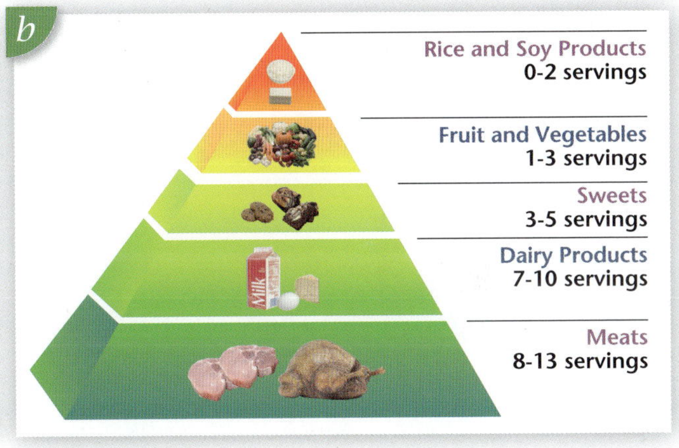

B. Multiple Choice

Circle the answer.

1. What is the main idea of the reading?
   - **a.** Okinawa consists of many islands.
   - **b.** People in Okinawa live longer.
   - **c.** Don't eat too many dairy products.
   - **d.** Only eat until you're 80 percent full.

2. What does **life expectancy** mean in the first paragraph?
   - **a.** how long people live
   - **b.** living over 86 years old
   - **c.** life on a small island
   - **d.** an age people expect to live

UNIT 11

Meet the Adélie Penguin

There are 18 kinds of penguins. They are in the bird family, but cannot fly. They spend most of their time near water. Penguins are also great swimmers. They can swim 200 meters underwater.

THINK ABOUT IT

Discuss with a partner.

1. How are penguins different from other birds?

2. What do you know about global warming?

3. How is global warming affecting the world in general?

4. Which animals will be hurt the most by global warming?

Before We Read

A. Read and Answer

Adélie **penguins** are the smallest penguins in the **Antarctic**. They are black and white. They look like they're wearing a **tuxedo**. When they walk, their long **tails** touch the ground. The tails help them when they are **diving** for fish. Adélie penguins can jump right out of the water onto the land. A group can have from 200 to 500,000 birds.

Write the words in bold above in the appropriate space. Change the form of the words if necessary.

	Word	Definition
1		to swim underwater
2		the back part of some animals' bodies
3		the most southern part of the world
4		a black and white sea bird
5		a man's jacket for formal events

B. Make Predictions

Read the title on page 92. What do you think the reading is about?

- ☐ the Adélie penguin: the fastest bird in the world
- ☐ opinions about tuxedos
- ☐ general information about a kind of penguin
- ☐ different kinds of penguins that are very fast

C. Scan

Read the article on page 92. Write the name of each animal.

1. 

s______________

2. 

k______________

3. 

s______________

4. 

s______________

Now Let's Read

Little Men in Tuxedos

Adélie Penguins: Fast Facts

Adélie penguins live in the Antarctic in groups. These groups can include thousands of birds.

Type: Bird

Diet: Fish & krill

Life Expectancy: Up to 20 years

Size: 45 – 75 cm

Weight: 3.9 – 5.8 kg

Biggest Enemy: Leopard seals

Did You Know . . .? Adélie penguins can hold their breath for two to three minutes.

Adélie penguins usually live on rocky beaches near the ice. This is where they build their nests, lay their eggs, and raise their babies. Their nests are made with rocks. Sometimes, Adélie penguins fight with their neighbors or steal rocks from them to get the best stones for their nests.

Both male and female Adélie penguins help to raise their babies. They take turns sitting on the eggs to keep them warm and safe. After they are three weeks old, parents are able to leave the baby penguins alone. Young penguins begin to swim on their own when they are nine weeks old.

Adélie penguins feed on the small, shrimp-like krill, but they also eat fish and squid. They usually hunt in shallow water, but they may travel as far as 300 kilometers in search of food. Adélie penguins are strong swimmers and have been known to dive as deep as 175 meters.

Comprehension Check

A. True or False

*Check **True** or **False**.*

	True	False
1. Adélie penguins prefer to hunt for food in deep water.	☐	☐
2. Leopard seals usually stay away from Adélie penguins.	☐	☐
3. Adélie penguins use rocks to build their nests.	☐	☐
4. Adélie penguins sometimes fight with their neighbors to get the best stones.	☐	☐
5. Only female Adélie penguins take care of their babies.	☐	☐
6. Adélie penguins are known as strong swimmers.	☐	☐

B. Fill in the Blanks

Complete the sentences with the words from the article.

1. Adélie penguins build their nests on the ____________ beaches of Antarctica.
2. Adélie penguins often try to ____________ rocks from other nests.
3. Male and female Adélie penguins take ____________ caring for their babies.
4. Adélie penguins ____________ on small fish, squid, and krill.
5. Adélie penguins are excellent swimmers. They're able to ____________ as deep as 175 meters.

C. Multiple Choice

Circle the answer.

1. How much do Adélie penguins weigh?
   a. for almost 20 years
   b. from about four to six kilograms
   c. just about 75 centimeters
   d. for two to three minutes

2. Where do Adélie penguins like to live?
   a. on rocky beaches
   b. in the water
   c. on the snow
   d. in the Arctic

3. What do Adélie penguins steal from their neighbors?
   a. food
   b. eggs
   c. nests
   d. rocks

4. Which of the following do Adélie penguins NOT eat?
   a. krill
   b. fish
   c. seals
   d. squids

5. What is true about Adélie penguins?
   a. They cannot swim very far in cold water.
   b. They can hold their breath for several minutes.
   c. They can swim on their own soon after they are born.
   d. They can fly when they are about nine weeks old.

Vocabulary Check

A. Word Definitions

Match the word/phrase with its definition.

Word	Definition
include •	• to eat
rocky •	• to have; to be made up of
steal •	• the kind of food you eat
feed on •	• to produce an egg
diet •	• covered with rocks
lay •	• to take someone else's things

B. Words with Different Meanings

Match the word in bold with its definition.

1 Penguins build their **nests** close together. ______
A lot of birds **nest** in trees. ______
Definition: ⓐ *n.* a place where birds live ⓑ *v.* to build a place for birds to live

2 Peter's father died when he was three. His mother **raised** him alone. ______
Lydia's boss gave her a **raise** because she worked hard. ______
Definition: ⓐ *v.* to help your child grow up ⓑ *n.* an increase in your salary

3 David's nose was broken in a **fight**. ______
Many people watched the two men **fighting**. ______
Definition: ⓐ *v.* to hit people ⓑ *n.* a physical conflict between people

C. Meanings in Context

Choose the meaning of the sentence.

1. **Thousands of** people want to work for the company.
   a. One thousand people want to work for the company.
   b. A large number of people want to work for the company.

2. Janice and I usually **take turns** cooking.
   a. Sometimes Janice cooks; sometimes I do.
   b. Janice and I usually cook together.

3. My sister won't **be able to** come tonight.
   a. My sister doesn't want to come tonight.
   b. My sister can't come tonight for some reason.

4. The man and his wife went out **in search of** their lost dog.
   a. The man and his wife went out to look for their lost dog.
   b. The man and his wife went out to pick up their lost dog.

Reading Strategy

Drawing Conclusions and Making Inferences

TIP

We practiced conclusions and inferences in Unit 3. Writers often tell us more than what they write. They do this by providing clues about the story that help us to read between the lines.

• Give It a Try •

PART I

Read and circle the appropriate inferences.

1. Adélie penguins live in the Antarctic in groups. These groups can include thousands of birds.
   - **a.** Adélie penguins are social animals.
   - **b.** Adélie penguins live longer than other birds.
   - **c.** Adélie penguins hold their breath for a long time.
   - **d.** The Adélie penguin is the smallest penguin.

2. Adélie penguins usually live on rocky beaches near the ice.
   - **a.** Adélie penguins like seals.
   - **b.** Adélie penguins are fat.
   - **c.** Adélie penguins can swim.
   - **d.** Adélie penguins are dangerous.

PART II

Read the passage and circle the answer.

I'm in my favorite place. It's a little loud, but **the sound of human voices** makes me feel good. I like coming here in the morning when all of the fruit and vegetables arrive. I always come early, so I can pick out something fresh to eat. There are other things here too. A woman is holding up a pair of earrings to her ears. Maybe I should buy some for my mom. <u>I don't care if it's crowded.</u> I love to be here because there is so much to see. This place is full of life.

1. What does **the sound of human voices** refer to?
   - **a.** a large group of people talking each other
   - **b.** a group of people who won't talk to each other
   - **c.** a person who makes a loud voice when he or she talks
   - **d.** a person who speaks a different language

2. What can we infer about the place with the underlined sentence?
   - **a.** People care about each other.
   - **b.** Many people visit this place.
   - **c.** It is convenient to visit this place.
   - **d.** This place is very peaceful.

3. Where do you think the writer might be?
   - **a.** at a hospital
   - **b.** at a school
   - **c.** at a playground
   - **d.** at a market

Further Reading

Save the Earth, Save Its Animals

Track 22

For many people, global warming is just something on the news. For animals around the world, it is something that affects their lives every day.

In Antarctica, the number of Adélie penguins has dropped in recent years. They need a long winter to hunt for food. However, the winter is now shorter and six degrees Celsius warmer. The penguins are also having trouble getting enough krill to eat. Because of this, the number of Adélie penguins has gone from 20,000 to only 4,000 in 35 years. Scientists think they may disappear completely in just ten years.

Animals in warm waters are hurt by global warming too. Coral reefs protect sea turtles and millions of colorful fish, such as clown fish and seahorses. The coral reef eats **algae**, but warmer ocean water changes the algae, and it becomes bad for the coral. When the coral dies, there is nothing to protect the beautiful animals living in it. Scientists believe that by 2050, the world's tropical* reefs and many of the animals that live in them will be gone.

Global warming is clearly a big problem, and animals everywhere are in danger. Humans need to live with animals. Therefore, we need to do something to make them a better home.

Reference:
* **tropical** *in the hottest parts of the world*

Comprehension Check

Extra Info

Coral reefs grow in water between 18 and 30 degrees Celsius. They are home to 25 percent of all sea life.

There are 28 kinds of **clown fish**. They are orange, yellow, blue, and many other colors.

Seahorses are true fish. Male seahorses give birth to babies and care for the young seahorses.

Adult **sea turtles** can actually weigh from 70 to 500 kilograms. Female turtles return to the place where they were born to lay their eggs.

A. Multiple Choice

Circle the answer.

1. How is global warming affecting Adélie penguins?
   - **a.** They are having more trouble hunting.
   - **b.** Krill are now starting to hunt them.
   - **c.** The ice is starting to increase.
   - **d.** The Antarctic summers become colder.

2. Which of the following is true?
   - **a.** There are 35 Adélie penguins left in Antarctica.
   - **b.** Reefs eat clown fish, seahorses, and sea turtles.
   - **c.** The number of Adélie penguins has dropped 80 percent.
   - **d.** Adélie penguins will disappear by 2050.

3. Coral reefs help to keep millions of fish ...
   - **a.** warm.
   - **b.** safe.
   - **c.** colorful.
   - **d.** cute.

4. What does **algae** refer to in the third paragraph?
   - **a.** ocean water that is changing
   - **b.** beautiful animals living in the reef
   - **c.** a thing that is harmful for the coral
   - **d.** something coral reefs feed on

5. From the **Extra Info** above, which of the following is true?
   - **a.** Coral reefs grow in water that is 25 degrees Celsius.
   - **b.** All sea life lives in coral reefs.
   - **c.** Female seahorses give birth.
   - **d.** A sea turtle weighs 1,000 kilograms.

UNIT 12 The Statue of Liberty

Quick Facts:

- *Her birthday is on October 28th.*
- *Visitors climb 354 stairs to get to the crown.*
- *People say the seven points on the crown are symbols for the seven continents.*
- *She weighs 204,117 kilograms.*

THINK ABOUT IT

Discuss with a partner.

1. What was the best birthday gift you have ever received or given?
2. Have you ever seen the Statue of Liberty in person? What did you feel?
3. How many landmarks have you visited?
4. What's the most beautiful landmark in the world?

Before We Read

A. Read and Answer

The Statue of Liberty in Paris

The Statue of **Liberty** is also known as Lady Liberty. It is a **symbol** of the United States' **separation** from England. It also marks the **friendship** between the people of France and America. But did you know that there is a copy in Paris? The copy is about 11 **meters** high. It was given to the French people in 1889 by Americans living in Paris. The statue faces west, toward its sister statue in New York City.

The Statue of Liberty stands on the island Île des Cygnes in the River Seine, Paris.

Write the words in bold above in the appropriate space. Change the form of the words if necessary.

	Word	Definition
1		a picture or shape that has a particular meaning
2		freedom
3		a relationship between friends
4		state of being separated
5		a unit for measuring length

B. Scan

Read the article on page 100. What do the following numbers refer to? There are two extra choices.

a. years that took the French to build the statue
b. the age of the United States in 1876
c. pieces the Statue of Liberty was broken into
d. people who helped build the Statue of Liberty
e. the weight of the Statue of Liberty
f. tourists who have visited the Statue of Liberty
g. the year the statue arrived in New York City
h. the height of the Statue of Liberty

1. 45 ______ 2. 204,117 ______ 3. 100 ______
4. 9 ______ 5. 350 ______ 6. 1885 ______

Now Let's Read

The World's Biggest Birthday Present

Who doesn't love birthdays? You get to eat birthday cake and get presents. But did you ever get a present that was over 45 meters high and weighed 204,117 kilograms? The United States did!

July 4th, 1876, was the 100th birthday of the United States. People in France wanted to mark this special day with a special present. A famous artist named Frédéric Bartholdi decided to make the United States a big birthday present — the Statue of Liberty.

It took Bartholdi and his workers a long time to build the statue. They worked ten hours a day, seven days a week for nine years! In June of 1884, the statue was finally complete. However, it was too big for any ship. To make it fit, they had to break it down into 350 pieces!

The statue arrived in New York City in 1885. Then it took four months to put the pieces back together. Today, the Statue of Liberty is one of the most popular tourist attractions in the city. More than five million people visit it every year.

The Statue of Liberty is more than just beautiful artwork or a big statue. It was created to celebrate the United States' separation from England 100 years earlier. It is also a symbol of friendship between France and America. Since then, the Statue of Liberty has welcomed many newcomers to New York City.

Comprehension Check

A. Main Idea

Write the number of the paragraph to match each topic.

1. the statue as a symbol ______
2. the size of the Statue of Liberty ______
3. the statue arriving in New York ______
4. the origin of the Statue of Liberty ______
5. building the statue ______

B. Put in Order

Put the following events in order.

a. The statue was taken apart.	**b.** New York City welcomed the Statue of Liberty.
c. The statue was put together again.	**d.** America turned 100 years old.
e. French people started building the statue.	**f.** The statue was completed in France.

______ → ______ → ______ → ______ → ______ → ______

C. Complete the Passage

Fill in the blanks with the words in the box. Change the form of the words if necessary.

friendship	present	fit	newcomer
tourist	piece	complete	symbol

In 1885, France gave America one of the biggest birthday ______________ ever, the Statue of Liberty. The statue was designed by a French artist and workers ______________ it in 1884. It wouldn't ______________ on a ship, so it had to be shipped in ______________. The statue is a ______________ of the two nations' ______________ and has welcomed a lot of ______________ to the United States. It is now one of New York's most popular ______________ spots.

D. Multiple Choice

Circle the answer.

1. What is the reading mainly about?
   a. the story of America's early days
   b. the history of the Statue of Liberty
   c. newcomers to New York City
   d. the famous artist Frédéric Bartholdi

2. The Statue of Liberty was ...
   a. built in four years.
   b. 100 meters high.
   c. difficult to ship.
   d. given by England.

3. Which of the following is NOT true?
   a. America's 100th birthday was July 4th, 1776.
   b. The statue weighs 204,117 kilograms.
   c. The statue arrived in New York in 1885.
   d. The statue was completed in 1884.

4. What can we say about the Statue of Liberty today?
   a. It will be broken down.
   b. It is one of the America's most popular destinations.
   c. It is not a symbol anymore.
   d. A famous American made it.

Vocabulary Check

A. Complete the Sentences

Fill in the blanks with the words in the box. Change the form of the words if necessary.

weigh	fit	piece	attraction	newcomer

1. Be careful! There is a ____________ of broken glass on the floor.
2. The beautiful beaches are the main ____________ of Florida.
3. Dave spent the morning showing the ____________ around the office.
4. I wanted to put the table next to the sofa, but I don't think it'll ____________.
5. The package ____________ more than 20 kilograms.

B. Words with Different Meanings

Match the word in bold with its definition.

1
At the **present** time, we have no plans for the weekend. ____
When Amy retired, the company **presented** her with a watch. ____
I bought Eva a special **present** for her birthday. ____
Definition: ⓐ *v.* to give ⓑ *adj.* current ⓒ *n.* a gift

2
The information is not **complete**. You forgot to write your phone number. ____
The house took three years to **complete**. ____
After hours of work, the boy's report was finally **complete**. ____
Definition: ⓐ *v.* to finish ⓑ *adj.* finished ⓒ *adj.* including everything

3
We try to make new workers feel **welcome**. ____
The man **welcomed** his guests at the door. ____
His parents gave him a warm **welcome** when he returned home. ____
Definition: ⓐ *n.* a greeting ⓑ *v.* to greet ⓒ *adj.* comfortable or wanted

C. Meanings in Context

Choose the meaning of the sentence.

1. The bed was **too** wide **for** the door.
   a. The bed was big and couldn't get through the door.
   b. The door was big and the bed was too small.

2. Terry **broke down** the table into five pieces.
   a. Terry put together the five parts of the table.
   b. Terry separated the table into five parts.

3. Sue is **more than just** a painter. She's also a musician.
   a. Sue likes painting more than playing music.
   b. Sue is both a painter and a musician.

4. You can see a lot of **artwork** in the room.
   a. There are many painters and photographers in the room.
   b. There are many paintings and photographs in the room.

Reading Strategy

Compound Nouns

TIP

Compound nouns usually have two parts. The two parts can be joined in several ways and be written as one word or two separate words. Look at the examples below:

- **Noun + Noun** ⇨ bed + room = bedroom
- **Noun + Verb** ⇨ hair + cut = haircut
- **Adjective + Noun** ⇨ black + board = blackboard
- **Verb + Noun** ⇨ swimming + pool = swimming pool

• Give It a Try •

PART I

Match the words in bold with the words on the right to make compound words.

birth •	• machine	1. ______________
art •	• pan	2. ______________
tourist •	• ache	3. ______________
washing •	• man	4. ______________
police •	• work	5. ______________
frying •	• day	6. ______________
new •	• attraction	7. ______________
head •	• comer	8. ______________

Use the compound words above to complete the sentences. Change the form of the words if necessary.

1. There are many ______________ to see in Los Angeles.
2. The ______________ still doesn't know how to use the fax machine.
3. More than 20 people came to Jan's ______________ party.
4. You can see a lot of nice ______________ in the museum.
5. Vince couldn't study because he had a bad ______________.

PART II

Read the passage and underline the compound words.

New York is a wonderful place to visit. There are a lot of different tourist spots. Any guidebook about New York will tell people how to get to places like Times Square, Central Park, and the Empire State Building. Here's a timetable to follow: In the morning, go shopping at one of the large department stores — Macy's or Barney's New York. In the afternoon, take a walk in the park or go to see a baseball game. In the evening, have a delicious dinner at a famous restaurant and then enjoy the interesting nightlife. One thing is for sure. You'll have a great time.

Further Reading

The Stories Behind Three Famous Landmarks*

Track 24

France

The Eiffel Tower has become the symbol of France. It was built as the entrance for the 1889 World's Fair. At that time, it was the tallest building in the world. But the people thought it was ugly and it was going to be taken apart. The city, however, decided to keep it. Over 100 years later, it's one of the most popular attractions in the world.

Italy

Pisa, Italy is famous for a mistake. The town started building a bell tower in 1173, but had to stop. One side was sinking, causing it to lean.* They tried to make it straight, but it just leaned the other way! In 1990, Pisa closed the tower to make it straighter. Now it is open again. The tower's still leaning, but this time it's not a mistake. And it's not in danger of falling.

India

Workers in India began building the Taj Mahal in 1632. The ruler wanted to remember his favorite wife among his wives — he had seven! The main dome* and its buildings were made out of marble.* When the ruler and his wife passed away, they were put inside the Taj Mahal, so the lovers could be together forever.

What landmark do people think of when you talk about your country? Do they say it's ugly? Is it about to fall down? Hopefully, you have a special place for it in your heart.

Reference:

- * **landmark** *a building or landscape that becomes famous*
- * **dome** *the round top on certain buildings*
- * **lean** *not to be straight; not to stand up*
- * **marble** *a hard rock that is used for making buildings*

Comprehension Check

A. Complete the Sentences

Fill in the blanks with the words in the box. Change the form of the words if necessary.

at that time	be taken apart	be famous for	in danger of
be made out of	pass away	be about to	fall down

1. The restaurant ______________ its Mexican food.
2. This desk ______________ wood.
3. Jeremy and his friends ______________ leave. It's six o'clock already.
4. Be careful on the wet floor! You might ______________.
5. Some of the furniture needs to ______________ before we dump it.
6. The old woman can't see very well. She's ______________ going blind.
7. I didn't like to eat vegetables ______________, but I do now.
8. My grandfather ______________ last year. He was 84 when he died.

B. Multiple Choice

Circle the answer.

1. What was the Eiffel Tower built for?
   a. the people of France
   b. the people of America
   c. the World's Fair
   d. the entrance to Paris

2. How did the people feel about the Eiffel Tower at first?
   a. They felt proud of it.
   b. They didn't like it.
   c. They were not interested in it.
   d. They wanted another.

3. Which of the following is true?
   a. People made Pisa straight.
   b. Pisa is in danger of falling these days.
   c. Pisa leaned when it was first built.
   d. Pisa was the tallest building in 1889.

4. Who did the ruler have the Taj Mahal built for?
   a. his favorite wife
   b. his workers
   c. his seven wives
   d. himself

5. What is NOT true about the Taj Mahal?
   a. It was made out of marble.
   b. It was completed in 1632.
   c. It was a kind of a tomb.
   d. It represented love.

NOTES

NOTES

AUDIO MP3 CONTENTS